WHERE STEEL WINDS BLOW

Where Steel Winds Blow

edited by ROBERT CROMIE

DAVID McKAY COMPANY, INC.
New York

WHERE STEEL WINDS BLOW

COPYRIGHT © 1968 BY ROBERT CROMIE

LIBRARY OF CONGRESS CATALOG CARD NUMBER: 68-57509

MANUFACTURED IN THE UNITED STATES OF AMERICA

VAN REES PRESS • NEW YORK

PREFACE

This anthology—the suggestion of Charles Molloy of David McKay—was intended, at first, simply as a collection of war poetry. But it quickly became apparent that the only war poems that appealed to me, with a few exceptions such as Vincent Starrett's dash-to-Paris one, were either noncommittal in their approach or violently anti-war.

Some of these poems, then, are forthright in their hatred of war. Others are quietly rebellious or wearily resigned, such as those by the poets of ancient China. And the overall effect, certainly, is not one of blaring bugles, waving banners, and the Light Brigade riding into the guns. In fact, you won't find the Light Brigade even hinted at anywhere but here.

I am not a pacifist. I doubt that most of the poets represented are pacifists. I believe that some wars are, at least in the end, justified and unavoidable. The only fault I find with our entry into World War II, for example (ignoring the obvious fact that Hitler should have been stopped years before by other means), is that it was too-long delayed. That struggle was both righteous and imperative. I believe the same thing could have been said if we had gone to the aid of some of Russia's unwilling satellites—notably Hungary, Poland, and Czechoslovakia—but that is another and equally unhappy story.

This disclaimer does not mean, however, that even in the case of a war against demons it is necessary for poets, or anyone else, to cherish war *itself*. War, regarded as an imponderable entity, a Thing that kills or maims, destroys people and cities, is lovingly allied with plague and famine, always is detestable and abhorrent even when it has to be embraced.

And in the case of a war that is reasonless, the horror is increased. It's tragic enough to kill or be killed in a war in which you believe. It is both tragic and diminishing to kill or be killed in a war that could have been prevented, a war that marches down a blood-drenched road to nowhere.

I feel that an anthology of this kind can be a valuable reminder that too many wars have been fought for the wrong reasons: empire, jingoism, a highly-selective portion of the national interest, perhaps to test new weapons (Spain may have been a case in point), because of a clash of religious beliefs, or for reasons no one can explain.

The poems included range widely both in time and in theme. They come from many countries. Some reject war completely, such as Thomas McGrath's taunting "Gone Away Blues," which begins:

> *Sirs, when you are in your last extremity,*
> *When your admirals are drowning in the grass-green sea,*
> *When your generals are preparing the total catastrophe—*
> *I just want you to know how you can not count on me.*

There are ones that mourn the lost future: "Mow down the young," says Edith Lovejoy Pierce. "Trample them under your boot." And there are those that regard the droning bombers with melancholy resignation: "A soulful nightingale enchants the park." Paul Scott Mowrer writes, "Ah, what a night! Ah, what a night to die!"

Bombing raids, in fact, have provided some of the most vivid protests. Louis MacNeice, telling of an attack on London, describes St. Paul's with its dome "riding the firefull night," and concludes, after telling of the blazing darkness and the coming of dawn, by saying: "So I . . . warmed my hands at London and went home."

There are the controlled but bitter outcries of those who have seen friends die: Sassoon's "I wish they'd killed you in a decent show." Or Wilfrid Wilson Gibson's "And stumbled blindly, muttering *Cheerio!* Into eternity, and left no trace." And the many verses that deal with the fate of the very old or the very

young in wartime, such as Charles Norman's final stanza of
"Footnote":

> *Our wars were chiefly*
> *Waged against children,*
> *Perpetual trudgers*
> *On endless newsreels.*

For the collection is by no means confined to the fighting men.
Scattered through the pages are hints of what war means to the
world in general—the music unwritten, the books that never will
see print, blueprints undrawn, children who never will be born.
Sometimes there is optimism:

"The corn outlasts the bayonet," says Humbert Wolfe. But he
also says, "For a lost flower is a little thing / But a lost lover
means the end of spring."

The irony and the anger are nothing new. From the 19th century comes Stephen Crane's:

> *Do not weep, maiden, for war is kind.*
> *Because your lover threw wild hands toward the sky*
> *And the affrighted steed ran on alone*
> *Do not weep.*
> *War is kind.*

And Longfellow, sounding a very modern note indeed:

> *Were half the power, that fills the world with terror,*
> *Were half the wealth bestowed on camps and courts,*
> *Given to redeem the human mind from error,*
> *There were no need of arsenals and forts.*

Elsewhere Witter Bynner suggests the possible aftermath of
some war-in-the-future in his closing for "The Old Men and the
Young Men":

> *Said the old men to the young men,*
> *"What is there left to do?"*
> *Said the young men to the old men,*
> *"You."*

This rebellion also is found in "Song for Heroes," by Alex Comfort, a British poet who wonders whether the ghosts of those slain in earlier wars would offer any advice beyond "Obedience is death," if they were to return.

There is no end to the variety of ideas. Edwin Rolfe has a fantasy of world-suicide in which both animate and inanimate objects destroy themselves in simultaneous mass protest, leaving only the soldiers alive: "Like forsaken chessmen abandoned by paralyzed players." Lindley William Hubbell comments on a visit to Hiroshima: ". . . we knew we were standing / Where the end of the world began." And David Mourao-Ferreira, upset at the bland indifference of his draft notice, complains: "—A tearstain would suffice / to give meaning to our death / convoked by your indifference!"

Finally, it is unrealistic to suppose that one more anthology will accomplish much. There have been anti-war poems in all ages, and things have changed little. But it is equally doubtful that anyone but the poet has been able to set down in such persuasive ways so exact a dissection of war and its impact on countries, persons, and the human soul. So another anthology is, I think, worth adding to the credit side of the ledger—wherever that ledger is kept.

ROBERT CROMIE

Chicago

ACKNOWLEDGMENTS

The Editor thanks the following publishing houses and individuals for their assistance.

"Prolonged Sonnet" by Niccolo Degli Albizzi. Reprinted courtesy of the Oxford University Press.

"Veteran," "Uncle Frank," and "Fascist Limericks" from *Rhyme and Punishment* by Leonard Bacon. Copyright © 1964 by Martha S. Bacon. Reprinted by permission of Holt, Rinehart & Winston, Inc.

"Prologue" from *Born to Flying Glass*, copyright © 1967, by Keith Barnes. Reprinted by permission of Harcourt, Brace & World, Inc.

"There Are No Good Giants" reprinted by permission of the publisher from *Never a Greater Need* by Walter Benton. Copyright 1948 by Alfred A. Knopf, Inc. "The Unknown Soldier" and "The Preview" reprinted by permission of the publisher from *Never a Greater Need* by Walter Benton. Copyright, 1946, 1948 by Alfred A. Knopf, Inc.

"Documentary" from *Poems and Epigrams by Robert Beum* (Regnery Chicago, 1964). Reprinted by permission of Henry Regnery Company.

"Exodus" from *Selected Poems of Jaime Torres Bodet* (Indiana University Press, 1964). Reprinted by permission of Indiana University Press.

"Gunnery Practice" copyright 1944 by John Malcolm Brinnin. From *The Selected Poems of John Malcolm Brinnin*. By permission of Atlantic-Little, Brown and Co.

"Five Ways to Kill a Man" from *With Love from Judas* by Edwin Brock. Reprinted by permission of Scorpion Press.

"Of the Great White War" from *The Song Book of Quong Lee of Limehouse* (Henry Holt and Co., New York). Copyright 1920 by Thomas Burke. Reprinted by permission of Paul R. Reynolds, Inc.

x   *Acknowledgments*

"An Old Man Reviews the Wars" and "The Old Men and the Young Men" reprinted by permission of Alfred A. Knopf, Inc. from *Book of Lyrics* by Witter Bynner. Copyright © 1955 by Witter Bynner.

"Nero's Term" by C. P. Cavafy. © 1961 by Rae Dalven. Reprinted from *The Complete Poems of Cavafy* translated by Rae Dalven by permission of Harcourt, Brace & World, Inc.

"Thinking of a Friend Lost in the Tibetan War" by Chang Chi. Reprinted by permission of the publisher from *The Jade Mountain* by Witter Bynner. Copyright, 1929 by Alfred A. Knopf, Inc. Renewed, 1957.

"Turkestan" by Ch'ên T'ao. Reprinted by permission of the publisher from *The Jade Mountain* by Witter Bynner. Copyright, 1929 by Alfred A. Knopf, Inc. Renewed, 1957.

"Among the Many Heaps of Ashes" by Cho Sung Kyun from *Poems from XV Languages* (The Stone Wall Press, Iowa City, Iowa, 1964).

"Elegy Just in Case" from *Other Skies* by John Ciardi. © 1947 Atlantic Monthly–Little Brown. "The Formalities" from *This Strangest Everything* by John Ciardi. © 1966, Rutgers, the State University. Both poems reprinted by permission of the author.

"Song for the Heroes" by Alex Comfort from *The Signal to Engage* (1946, Routledge & Kegan Paul Ltd.). Used by permission.

"The Choice" from *The Early Drowned* by Hilary Corke. Reprinted by permission from Martin Secker and Warburg Ltd.

"My Sweet Old Etcetera" by E. E. Cummings. Copyright, 1926, by Horace Liveright; copyright, 1954, by E. E. Cummings. Reprinted from *Poems 1923–1954* by permission of Harcourt, Brace & World, Inc. "plato told" by E. E. Cummings. Copyright, 1944, by E. E. Cummings. Reprinted from his volume, *Poems 1923–1954* by permission of Harcourt, Brace & World, Inc.

"The Roman Road" from *The Long Street* by Donald Davidson (Vanderbilt University Press, 1961).

"Only the Beards Are Different" by Bruce Dawe from *Poetry in Australia, Vol. II–Modern Australian Verse*, edited by Douglas Stewart, published by Angus & Robertson Ltd., 1964.

"Disasters of War: Goya at the Museum" by Babette Deutsch. Reprinted by permission of Curtis Brown, Ltd. Copyright © 1959 by Babette Deutsch.

"The Trumpet" by Keith Douglas from *Collected Poems*, edited by John Waller, G. S. Fraser and J. C. Hall. Copyright 1966 by Marie J. Douglas. Reprinted by permission of Chilmark Press. "Vergissmeinicht" and "John Anderson" from *Selected Poems—Keith Douglas*, edited, with an introduction by Ted Hughes. Copyright Marie J. Douglas, 1964. Reprinted by permission of Chilmark Press.

"International Conference" and "Spaniel's Sermons" by Colin Ellis from *Mournful Numbers, Verses and Epigrams* (Macmillan & Co., Ltd., London, 1932). Reprinted by permisson of the author.

"The Benediction: An Incident of the Spanish Civil War" from *Midnight in the Century* by Maurice English (The Prairie School Press, Park Forest, Illinois, 1964). Reprinted by permission of the author.

"The Hometown Hero Comes Home" from *Go Read the River* by Dave Etter (University of Nebraska Press, 1966). Reprinted by permission of the author.

"Attila" by William Everson from *Single Source, The Early Poems of William Everson, 1934–1940* (Oyez, Berkeley, California, 1966). Reprinted by permission of the author and the publishers.

"The Articles of War" from *Come Out into the Sun: Poems New and Selected* by Robert Francis, © 1965. Used by permission of The University of Massachusetts Press.

"On a Portrait by Copley" from *Appolonian Poems* by Arthur Freeman. Copyright © 1961, by Arthur Freeman. Reprinted by permission of Atheneum Publishers.

"Spring MCMXL" from *Collected Poems* by David Gascoyne, published by Oxford University Press. Reprinted by permission of Oxford University Press.

"Home" by Karen Gershon from *Selected Poems*. Copyright © 1966, by Karen Gershon. Reprinted by permission of Harcourt, Brace & World, Inc.

"In the Ambulance," "Breakfast," "The Joke," "Dick Milburn," and "Philip Dagg" from *Collected Poems 1905–1925* by Wilfrid Gibson. Reprinted by permission of Mr. Michael Gibson and Macmillan & Co. Ltd., London.

"On a Very Young, Very Dead Soldier" by Richard Gillman. Reprinted by permission of the publishers, Swallow Press, Inc., Chicago.

"The Persian Version" and "The Last Day of Leave (1916)" by Robert Graves from *Collected Poems* (Doubleday & Company, 1955). Copyright © 1955, by Robert Graves. Reprinted by permission of Collins-Knowlton-Wing, Inc. "Escape" by Robert Graves. Copyright © 1917, by Robert Graves. Reprinted by permission of Collins-Knowlton-Wing, Inc.

"Death and General Putnam" from the book *Death and General Putnam and 101 Other Poems* by Arthur Guiterman. Copyright 1935, by E. P. Dutton & Co., Inc. Renewal © 1963, by Mrs. Vida Lindo Guiterman. Reprinted by permission of the publishers.

"Achtung! Achtung!" by Mary Hacker from *New Poems 1963: A British P.E.N. Anthology* edited by Lawrence Durrell, © 1963 by P.E.N. Reprinted by permission of Harcourt, Brace & World, Inc.

"The Old Pilot's Death" and "An Airstrip in Essex, 1960" by Donald Hall. Reprinted by permission of Curtis Brown, Ltd. Copyright © 1964 by Donald Hall.

"Christmas: 1924" by Thomas Hardy. Reprinted with permission of The Macmillan Company from *Winter Words* by Thomas Hardy. Copyright 1928 by Florence E. Hardy and Sydney E. Cockerell, renewed 1956 by Lloyd's Bank Ltd. "The Man He Killed" by Thomas Hardy. Reprinted with permission of The Macmillan Company from *Collected Poems* by Thomas Hardy. Copyright 1925 by The Macmillan Company.

"No Quarrel" from *Siren Song* by A. P. Herbert. Copyright 1939 by Alan Patrick Herbert. Used by permission of Doubleday & Company, Inc. "France" and "These Are the Boys" from *Siren Song* by A. P. Herbert. Copyright 1940 by Alan Patrick Herbert. Used by permission of Doubleday & Company, Inc.

"The Voices of Peace Are Hushed" from *In the Month of Green Fire, New and Collected Poems* by Sophie Himmell (Arco, New York, 1964). Reprinted by permission of the publishers.

"In Humbleness" by Daniel G. Hoffman from *An Armada of Thirty Whales*. Copyright 1954 by Yale University Press. Reprinted by permission.

"The Sergeant Major," "A Survivor," and "Innocents" from *Collected Poems, 1935–1965* by Kenneth Hopkins. Copyright © 1964, by Kenneth Hopkins. Reprinted by permission of the Southern Illinois University Press.

"Reviewing Negro Troops Going South Through Washington, April 26, 1864," "Pinned Down," and "Commander Death" by Paul Horgan. Reprinted with the permission of Farrar, Straus & Giroux, Inc., from *Songs After Lincoln* by Paul Horgan. Copyright © 1960, 1965 by Paul Horgan.

"The Day of Battle" by A. E. Housman from *A Shropshire Lad—Authorized Edition—*frrom *The Collected Poems of A. E. Housman.* Copyright 1939, 1940; © 1959 by Holt, Rinehart and Winston, Inc. Copyright © 1967 by Robert E. Symons. Reprinted by permission of Holt, Rinehart and Winston, Inc. "XXXVII" and "XXXVI" from *The Collected Poems of A. E. Housman.* Copyright 1936 by Barclays Bank Ltd. Copyright © 1964 by Robert E. Symons. Reprinted by permission of Holt, Rinehart and Winston, Inc.

"The Locust Swarm" by Hsu Chao from Kenneth Rexroth, *One Hundred Poems from the Chinese.* All Rights Reserved. Reprinted by permission of New Directions Publishing Corporation.

"At Hiroshima" by Lindley Williams Hubbell. Reprinted by permission of the publishers, Swallow Press, Inc., Chicago.

"Without Benefit of Declaration" reprinted by permission of Alfred A. Knopf, Inc., from *The Panther and the Lash* by Langston Hughes. Copyright 1967 by Langston Hughes.

"The Death of the Ball Turret Gunner" by Randall Jarrell. Reprinted with permission of Mrs. Randall Jarrell. Copyright 1967.

"The Bloody Sire" by Robinson Jeffers. Copyright 1941 by Robinson Jeffers. Reprinted from *Selected Poems,* by Robinson Jeffers, by permission of Random House, Inc.

"The Last Campaign" by Geoffrey Lehmann from *Poetry in Australia, Vol. II—Modern Australian Verse,* edited by Douglas Stewart, published by Angus & Robertson Ltd., 1964.

"The Spires of Oxford" from the book *The Spires of Oxford and Other Poems* by Winifred M. Letts. Copyright, 1917, by E. P. Dutton & Co., Inc. Renewal, 1945, by Winifred M. Letts. Reprinted by permission of the publishers.

"What Were They Like?" from Denise Levertov, *The Sorrow Dance.* © 1966 by Denise Levertov Goodman. Reprinted by permission of New Directions Publishing Corporation.

"The Moon at the Fortified Pass" by Li Po. Reprinted by permission of the publisher from *The Jade Mountain* by Witter Bynner. Copyright, 1929, by Alfred A. Knopf, Inc. Renewed, 1957. "The Nefarious War" by Li Po from the book *The Works of Li Po* translated by Shigeyoshi Obata. Copyright 1922; renewal, 1950, by E. P. Dutton & Co., Inc. Reprinted by permission of the publishers.

"Misericordia" from *Pictures of the Floating World* by Amy Lowell (Houghton Mifflin, 1919). Reprinted by permission of the publishers. "Patterns" by Amy Lowell from *Men, Women and Ghosts* (Houghton Mifflin, 1916). Reprinted by permission of the publishers.

"Before the Charge (Loos, 1915)" from the book *Soldier Songs* by Patrick MacGill. Published by E. P. Dutton & Co., Inc. and reprinted with their permission.

"Homage to Wren (a memory of 1941)" from *The Collected Poems of Louis MacNeice,* edited by E. R. Dodds. Copyright © The Estate of Louis MacNeice, 1966. Reprinted by permission of Oxford University Press, Inc.

"Sonnet: To the Castle at Gordes" by Olivier de Magny from *Poems of War Resistance 1966 Peace Calendar* (War Resisters League, New York, 1966). Reprinted with the permission of Scott Bates.

"The Bayonet" and "The Butchers at Prayer" from *Dreams and Dust* by Don Marquis. Copyright 1915 by Harper & Bros. Reprinted by permission of Doubleday & Company, Inc.

"Dido of Tunisia" and "Soldier Asleep" from *Times Three* by Phyllis McGinley. Copyright 1943 by Phyllis McGinley. Originally appeared in *The New Yorker.* Reprinted by permission of The Viking Press, Inc.

"Remembering That Island" and "Gone Away Blues" by Thomas McGrath reprinted by permission of the publishers, Swallow Press, Inc., Chicago.

"And Then There Were None" by Edna St. Vincent Millay from *Make Bright the Arrows,* Harper & Row. Copyright 1940 by Edna St. Vincent Millay. "Czecho-Slovakia" by Edna St. Vincent Millay from *Collected Poems,* Harper & Row. Copyright 1939, 1967 by Edna St. Vincent Millay and Norma Millay Ellis. "Conscientious Objector" by Edna St. Vincent Millay from *Collected Poems,* Harper & Row. Copyright 1934, 1962 by Edna St. Vincent Millay and Norma Millay Ellis.

"The Kings Are Passing Deathward," "Napoleon in Hades," and "The School Boy Reads His Iliad" from *Ships in Harbour* by David Morton (G. P. Putnam's Sons, New York and London, 1921).

"Communiqué from an Army Deserter Probably Italian" reprinted with permission of The Macmillan Company from *The Wrong Angel* by Stanley Moss. © Stanley Moss 1963.

"Draft Notice" by David Mourão-Ferreira from *Selections from Contemporary Portuguese Poetry: A Bilingual Selection,* by Jean R. Longland. © 1966 by Harvey House, Inc. by permission of Evelyn Singer and Harvey House.

"Pastoral" and "Night Bombers" by Paul Scott Mowrer from *The Mothering Land: Selected Poems (1918–1958)* (Golden Quill Press, Francestown, N.H., 1960).

"Black Douglas" from *Balm in Gilead* by Helene Mullins. Copyright 1930 by Harper & Brothers; renewed 1958 by Helene Mullins. Reprinted by permission of Harper & Row, Publishers.

"A Letter from the Front" from *Poems New and Old* by Sir Henry Newbolt (A. P. Watt & Son). Reprinted by permission of Mr. Peter Newbolt.

Poems by Charles Norman: "Epitaph for a Leader," "The Moors Fight on the Side of God," "Portrait of a Senator," and "Lovers, Forget the Moon" reprinted with permission of The Macmillan Company from *Selected Poems* by Charles Norman. Copyright 1942 by The Macmillan Company. "Footnote" reprinted with permission of The Macmillan Company from *Selected Poems* by Charles Norman. © Stanley Moss 1957. "Speech by Moonlight" and "To Another Poet a Thousand Years Hence" reprinted with permission of The Macmillan Company from *Selected Poems* by Charles Norman. © Stanley Moss 1962. "Triumphal Entry" reprinted with permission of The Macmillan Company from *Selected Poems* by Charles Norman. Copyright 1939 by Charles Norman, renewed 1967 by Charles Norman. "The Savage Century" reprinted with permission of The Macmillan Company from *Selected Poems* by Charles Norman. Copyright 1937 by Charles Norman, renewed 1965 by Charles Norman. Originally appeared in *The New Yorker*. "For and Against" reprinted with permission of The Macmillan Company from *Selected Poems* by Charles Norman. Copyright 1945 by Charles Norman. Reprinted from *Mademoiselle*. "Death, Look to Your Domain" reprinted with permission of The Macmillan Company from

Selected Poems by Charles Norman. Copyright 1943 by Charles Norman. Originally appeared in *The New Yorker.*

"The Send-Off," "Anthem for Doomed Youth," "Strange Meeting," "The Last Laugh," and "Dulce et Decorum Est" from *Wilfred Owen, Collected Poems.* ⓒ 1963 by Chatto & Windus, Ltd. Reprinted by permission of New Directions Publishing Corporation.

"War Song" from *The Portable Dorothy Parker.* Copyright 1944 by Dorothy Parker. Originally appeared in *The New Yorker.* Reprinted by permission of The Viking Press, Inc.

"To the Warmakers," "Patterns," "Ruins," "Beethoven's Ninth Symphony in Wartime," "Music Room," "Sic Transit Gloria," "Heartbreak Ridge," and "Great Powers Conference" by Edith Lovejoy Pierce. Reprinted by permission of the author.

"For Carlos, at War" by Merle Price from *A Time for Poetry* (John F. Blair, 1966). Reprinted by permission of The North Carolina Poetry Society and the author.

"The Happy Warrior" and "The Refugees" from *Collected Poems* by Herbert Read, copyright 1966, by permission of the publishers, Horizon Press, New York.

"Naming of Parts" by Henry Reed from *A Map of Verona and Other Poems.* Copyright 1947, by Henry Reed. Reprinted by permission of Harcourt, Brace & World, Inc.

"On a Military Graveyard" from *Collected Shorter Poems* by Kenneth Rexroth. Copyright 1956 by New Directions. Reprinted by permission of New Directions Publishing Corporation.

"Trench Poets" by Edgell Rickword from *Oxford Poetry 1921,* edited by Alan Porter, Richard Hughes, Robert Graves (D. Appleton and Co., New York, 1923). Reprinted by permission of the author.

"A Poem to Delight My Friends Who Laugh at Science-Fiction" by Edwin Rolfe reprinted by permission of the Editor of *Poetry,* copyright 1953, The Modern Poetry Association.

"Futurama Love Song" and "Harry" from the book, *Thrive Upon the Rock,* by Norman Rosten. Copyright ⓒ 1965 by Norman Rosten. Reprinted by permission of Trident Press.

"Grass" from *Cornhuskers* by Carl Sandburg. Copyright 1918 by Holt, Rinehart and Winston, Inc. Copyright 1946 by Carl Sandburg. Reprinted by permission of Holt, Rinehart and Winston, Inc.

"The General," "Base Details," "Dreamers," "Counter-Attack," "The Effect," "The Investiture," "To Any Dead Officer," "Survivors," "Lamentations," and "Fight to a Finish" from *Collected Poems* by Siegfried Sassoon. Copyright 1918 by E. P. Dutton & Co.; 1946 by Siegfried Sassoon. Reprinted by permission of The Viking Press, Inc. "At Carnoy" and "They" from *Collected Poems* by Siegfried Sassoon. Copyright 1918 by E. P. Dutton & Co. All rights reserved. Reprinted by permission of The Viking Press, Inc.

"I Have a Rendezvous with Death" from *Poems* by Alan Seeger. Copyright 1916 by Charles Scribner's Sons; renewal copyright 1944 by Elsie Adams Seeger. Reprinted with the permission of Charles Scribner's Sons.

"Untitled Sonnet" by Joseph Seligman reprinted from *The Last Great Cause* by Stanley Weintraub, published by Weybright and Talley, 1968. Reprinted by permission of Stanley Weintraub of Pennsylvania State University.

"Lines" by Shên Ch'üan-ch'i reprinted by permission of the publisher from *The Jade Mountain* by Witter Bynner. Copyright 1929 by Alfred A. Knopf, Inc. Renewed, 1957.

"The Ash and the Oak" from *Good News of Death and Other Poems* by Louis Simpson, Poets of Today II (copyright 1951 by Louis Simpson). Reprinted with the permission of Charles Scribner's Sons. "Black Kettle Raises the Stars and Stripes" by Louis Simpson from *Selected Poems*, copyright © 1965, by Louis Simpson. Reprinted by permission of Harcourt, Brace & World, Inc. "The Battle" reprinted with the permission of Charles Scribner's Sons from *Good News of Death and Other Poems* by Louis Simpson (copyright 1955 by Louis Simpson), Poets of Today II. "The Heroes" from *Good News of Death and Other Poems* by Louis Simpson, Poets of Today II (copyright 1950 by Louis Simpson). Reprinted with the permission of Charles Scribner's Sons.

"Beach Burial" by Kenneth Slessor from *Poetry in Australia, Vol. II—Modern Australian Verse*, edited by Douglas Stewart, published by Angus & Robertson Ltd., 1964.

"Of Late" from *White Paper* by George Starbuck. Copyright © 1960, 1961, 1962, 1963, 1964, 1965, 1966 by George Starbuck. Reprinted by permission of Atlantic-Little, Brown and Co.

"D'Artagnan" reprinted by permission of the author, Vincent Starrett. From *Estrays*, 2d ed. (Bookfellows, Chicago, 1920).

"Newsreel in Wartime" by Adrien Stoutenburg from *The Wind Listens, An Anthology of Contemporary Poetry,* edited and with an introduction by Marjorie Peters (The Dierkes Press, Chicago, 1953). Reprinted by permission of Marjorie Peters.

"Return to Hiroshima" by Lucien Stryk. Reprinted by permission of the publishers, Swallow Press, Inc., Chicago.

"A Boy" and "There Will Come Soft Rains" reprinted with permission of The Macmillan Company from *Flame and Shadow* by Sara Teasdale. Copyright 1920 by The Macmillan Company, renewed 1948 by Mamie T. Wheless. "Dusk in War Time" reprinted with permission of The Macmillan Company from *Love Songs* by Sara Teasdale. Copyright 1915 by The Macmillan Company, renewed 1943 by Mamie T. Wheless.

"Lincolnshire Bomber Station," "To Certain Ladies, on Going to the Wars," "In the Third Year of War," and "War Poem" reprinted by permission of Alfred A. Knopf, Inc. from *Collected Poems* by Henry Treece. Copyright 1946 by Henry Treece.

"Thermopylae 1941" from *Grooves in the Wind* by C. A. Trypanis. Copyright 1964 by C. A. Trypanis. Reprinted by permission of Chilmark Press.

"Both Sides of the Yellow River Recaptured by the Imperial Army" and "A Song of War Chariots" by Tu Fu reprinted, by permission of the publisher, from *The Jade Mountain* by Witter Bynner. Copyright 1929 by Alfred A. Knopf, Inc. Renewed, 1957. "Official Visit to Shih Hao Village" by Tu Fu reprinted by permission of Scott Bates.

"Two Funerals" by Louis Untermeyer. Copyright 1914, by Harcourt, Brace & World, Inc.; copyright 1942, by Louis Untermeyer. Reprinted from *Long Feud* by Louis Untermeyer, by permission of Harcourt, Brace & World, Inc.

" 'Vale' from Carthage (Spring, 1944)" by Peter Viereck. Copyright by Peter Viereck from his *New and Selected Poems,* New York, Bobbs Merrill Company, 1967.

"On the Death of a Murderer" from *Weep Before God: Poems by John Wain.* Reprinted by permission of St. Martin's Press, Inc., Macmillan & Co., Ltd. of London, and Macmillan & Company, Ltd. of Canada.

"A Son of Liang-Chou" by Wang Han reprinted by permission of the publisher from *The Jade Mountain* by Witter Bynner. Copyright 1929 by Alfred A. Knopf, Inc. Renewed, 1957.

"War in Chang-An City" by Wang Tsan reprinted by permission of Scott Bates.

"The Mound in the Meads" from *The Poems of Sir William Watson 1878–1935*, George G. Harrap & Co., Ltd., London.

"Earth (with apologies to *The New Yorker*)" by John Hall Wheelock from *The Gardener and Other Poems* by John Hall Wheelock (Copyright © 1961 by John Hall Wheelock). Reprinted by permission of Charles Scribner's Sons.

"Reflections upon a Recurrent Suggestion by Civil Defense Authorities that I build a Bombshelter in My Backyard" from *An American Takes a Walk and Other Poems* by Reed Whittemore, University of Minnesota Press, Minneapolis. © 1956 by Reed Whittemore.

"On the Eyes of an SS Officer" and "Mined Country" by Richard Wilbur from *The Beautiful Changes and Other Poems*, copyright 1947, by Richard Wilbur. Reprinted by permission of Harcourt, Brace & World, Inc. "Shame," © 1961 by Richard Wilbur. Reprinted from his volume *Advice to a Prophet and Other Poems* by permission of Harcourt, Brace & World, Inc.

"For Lover Man, and All the Other Young Men Who Failed to Return from World War II" by Mance Williams from *New Negro Poets, USA*, edited by Langston Hughes (Indiana University Press, 1964). Reprinted by permission of Indiana University Press.

"Flowers at Hampton Court," "France," and "V.D.F. (Ave atque Vale)," by Humbert Wolfe, used by permission.

"Frontier Guard" by Tom Wright from *Best Poems of 1957*, Borestone Mountain Poetry Awards 1958, Robert T. Moore, Editor in Chief (Stanford University Press, 1958).

"They Say the Last Supper Is Badly Damaged" by Samuel Yellen from *New and Selected Poems* (Indiana University Press, 1964). Reprinted by permission of Indiana University Press.

"The Companion" by Yevgeny Yevtushenko from *Selected Poems*, translated with an introduction by Robin-Milner-Gulland and Peter Levi, S.J. (Penguin Books, Baltimore, 1962).

"Fighting South of the Castle" reprinted by permission of the publisher from *Translations from the Chinese,* by Arthur Waley. Copyright 1919 by Alfred A. Knopf, Inc. Renewed, 1947, by Arthur Waley.

"I Sit with My Dolls" translated by Joseph Leftwich, reprinted from *Commentary,* by permission; copyright © 1951 by the American Jewish Committee.

At McKay, the editor wishes to give grateful thanks to Howard Cady, to Alyss Dorese, and especially to Elizabeth O'Neil, who helped tremendously in getting permissions and in putting the manuscript together.

CONTENTS

WHERE STEEL WINDS BLOW

ACHTUNG! ACHTUNG!

I'm war. Remember me?
"Yes, you're asleep," you say, "and you kill men,"
Look in my game-bag, fuller than you think.

I kill marriages.
If one dies, one weeps and then heals clean.
(No scar without infection.) That's no good.
I can do better when I really try.
I wear down the good small faiths, enough
For little strains of peace, the near, the known,
But not for the big absence, man-sized silences,
Family pack of dangers, primate lusts
I hang on them.

I kill families.
Cut off the roots, the plant will root no more.
Tossed from thin kindness to thin kindness on
The child grows no more love; will only seek
A pinchbeck eros and a tawdry shock.
I teach the race to dread its unborn freak.
I maim well.

I drink gold.
How kind of you to pour it without stint
Into my sleeping throat. In case I die?
You think I'm god, the one that pours the most
Getting my sanction? Well, perhaps you're right.
Divert it, anyway, from use of peace;
Keep the gross gaol, starvation and the lout,
The succulent tumour, loving bacillus, the clot
As bright as mine, friends all. I pop their prey
Into my bag.

I am the game that nobody can win.
What's yours is mine, what's mine is still my own.
I'm War. Remember me.

MARY HACKER

CHRISTMAS: *1924*

"Peace upon earth!" was said. We sing it,
And pay a million priests to bring it.
After two thousand years of mass
We've got as far as poison-gas.

THOMAS HARDY

AN OLD MAN REVIEWS THE WARS

Which war is it?
I cannot seem to tell.
There have been so many,
And none has turned out well.

Who fights for whom?
Toward whom are we a foe?
It seems to make no difference,
Now or long ago.

WITTER BYNNER

THE ASH AND THE OAK

When men discovered freedom first
The fighting was on foot,
They were encouraged by their thirst
And promises of loot,
And when it feathered and bows boomed
Their virtue was a root.

O the ash and the oak and the willow tree
And green grows the grass on the infantry!

At Malplaquet and Waterloo
They were polite and proud,
They primed their guns with billets-doux
And, as they fired, bowed.
At Appomattox too, it seems,
Some things were understood.

O the ash and the oak and the willow tree
And green grows the grass on the infantry!

But at Verdun and at Bastogne
There was a great recoil,
The blood was bitter to the bone
The trigger to the soul,
And death was nothing if not dull,
A hero was a fool.

O the ash and the oak and the willow tree
And that's an end of the infantry!

LOUIS SIMPSON

ATTILA

On a low Lorranian knoll a leaning peasant sinking a pit
Meets rotted rock and a slab.
The slab cracks and is split, the old grave opened,
His spade strikes iron and keenly rings.
Out of the earth he picks an ancient sword,
Hiltless with rust and the blade a long double curve,
Steel of no Roman nor Teuton king,
But metal struck in the sleeping East and lost in the raids.
He turns it awhile in the thick hands,
His thumb searching the eaten edge, and throws it aside.
The brown strip winks in the light and is sunk,
Winks once in a thousand years, in the sun and the singing air,
And is lost again in the ground.

Attila, you rode your hordes from the Asian slopes and swept to
    the west,
Roaring down Rome and the north-born Goths.
In the screaming dawns you struck the rich earth and left it
    smoking;
Struck and butchered and lived like the crimson arc of a cutting
    knife.
Through the reeling years you ran like a wolf,
Side-slashing blindly from border to border the length of that
    bleeding land,
Till your own lust killed you and the dark swarm broke.

In the nights the moon crawls to the west and is hidden;
The dawns bloom in the east;
The fogs gather.

Attila, in your frenzy of life you burned, but for nothing.
You roared for an instant, shook the world's width, broke the
    fierce tribes.

You are outdone: the earth that you raped has been ravaged
   more foully;
The cities you sacked have been burnt and rebuilt a hundred
   times;
From your day to this the valleys you plundered
Have known killing and looting, the sharp violence,
The running thunder shaking the night,
A gasping moment of peace and then at it again!

Yet you struck deep: in the fields the earth gives up a curious
   sword;
The bright-haired folk of a German farm
Regard with doubt a baby born with oval eyes;
In a gusty hut an old man hugs the hearth
And tells an ancient story.

WILLIAM EVERSON

THE LOCUST SWARM

Locusts laid their eggs in the corpse
Of a soldier. When the worms were
Mature, they took wing. Their drone
Was ominous, their shells hard.
Anyone could tell they had hatched
From an unsatisfied anger.
They flew swiftly towards the North.
They hid the sky like a curtain.
When the wife of the soldier
Saw them, she turned pale, her breath
Failed her. She knew he was dead
In battle, his corpse lost in
The desert. That night she dreamed
She rode a white horse, so swift
It left no footprints, and came

To where he lay in the sand.
She looked at his face, eaten
By the locusts, and tears of
Blood filled her eyes. Ever after
She would not let her children
Injure any insect which
Might have fed on the dead. She
Would lift her face to the sky
And say, "O locusts, if you
Are seeking a place to winter,
You can find shelter in my heart."

HSU CHAO

AMONG THE MANY HEAPS OF ASHES

My native town turned
Into many heaps of ashes.

As in a sudden nightmare
I walked through the rubble
Looking for the place
Where the house had stood in which I was born.

The small road leading
To my playmates' houses
Is gone.
The apricot tree in Young Za's yard
Is no longer there.
And on the heaps of ashes
The grass is taller than I am.

I am standing among
The heaps of ashes
And the army trucks go past
Leaving trails of dust.

The surrounding mountains in the distance
Are familiar to my eyes.
But I cannot believe
This town was so peaceful once—
With small houses and sandy brooks
Full of playing children.

As in a story I am standing
Among the grassy heaps of ashes.
And I understand
The fairy tales I read and heard
Might have existed once
Like the days of childhood
In the small corners of
My lost house, my town.

CHO SUNG KYUN
Korea

FIGHTING SOUTH OF THE CASTLE

They fought south of the Castle,
They died north of the wall.
They died in the moors and were not buried.
Their flesh was the food of crows.
"Tell the crows we are not afraid;
We have died in the moors and cannot be buried.
Crows, how can our bodies escape you?"
The waters flowed deep
And the rushes in the pool were dark.
The riders fought and were slain:
Their horses wander neighing.
By the bridge there was a house.
Was it south, was it north?
The harvest was never gathered.
How can we give you your offerings?

You served your Prince faithfully,
Though all in vain.
I think of you, faithful soldiers;
Your service shall not be forgotten.
For in the morning you went out to battle
And at night you did not return.

ANONYMOUS

THINKING OF A FRIEND LOST
IN THE TIBETAN WAR

Last year you went with your troops to Tibet;
And when your men had vanished beyond the city-wall,
News was cut off between the two worlds
As between the living and the dead.
No one has come upon a faithful horse guarding
A crumpled tent or torn flag, or any trace of you.
If only I knew, I might serve you in the temple,
Instead of these tears toward the far sky.

CHANG CHI

TURKESTAN

Thinking only of their vow that they would crush the Tartars—
On the desert, clad in sable and silk, five thousand of them
    fell . . .
But arisen from their crumbling bones on the banks of the river
    at the border,
Dreams of them enter, like men alive, into rooms where their
    loves lie sleeping.

CH'ÊN T'AO

THE MOON AT THE FORTIFIED PASS
(Written to Music)

The bright moon lifts from the Mountain of Heaven
In an infinite haze of cloud and sea,
And the wind, that has come a thousand miles,
Beats at the Jade Pass battlements. . . .
China marches its men down Po-têng Road
While Tartar troops peer across blue waters of the bay . . .
And since not one battle famous in history
Sent all its fighters back again,
The soldiers turn round, looking toward the border,
And think of home, with wistful eyes,
And of those tonight in the upper chambers
Who toss and sigh and cannot rest.

LI PO

LINES

Against the City of the Yellow Dragon
Our troops were sent long years ago,
And girls here watch the same melancholy moon
That lights our Chinese warriors—
And young wives dream a dream of spring,
That last night their heroic husbands,
In a great attack, with flags and drums,
Captured the City of the Yellow Dragon.

SHÊN CH'ÜAN-CH'I

BOTH SIDES OF THE YELLOW RIVER
RECAPTURED BY THE IMPERIAL ARMY

News at this far western station! The north has been recaptured!
At first I cannot check the tears from pouring on my coat—
Where is my wife? Where are my sons?
Yet crazily sure of finding them, I pack my books and poems—
And loud my song and deep my drink
On the green spring-day that starts me home,
Back from this mountain, past another mountain,
Up from the south, north again—to my own town!

Tu Fu

A SONG OF WAR CHARIOTS
(Written to Music)

The war chariots rattle,
The war-horses whinny.
Each man of you has a bow and a quiver at his belt.
Father, mother, son, wife, stare at you going,
Till dust shall have buried the bridge beyond Ch'ang-an.
They run with you, crying, they tug at your sleeves,
And the sound of their sorrow goes up to the clouds;
And every time a bystander asks you a question,
You can only say to him that you have to go.
... We remember others at fifteen sent north to guard the river
And at forty sent west to cultivate the camp-farms.
The mayor wound their turbans for them when they started out.
With their turbaned hair white now, they are still at the border,
At the border where the blood of men spills like the sea—
And still the heart of Emperor Wu is beating for war.

. . . Do you know that, east of China's mountains, in two hun-
dred districts
And in thousands of villages, nothing grows but weeds,
And though strong women have bent to the ploughing,
East and west the furrows all are broken down?
. . . Men of China are able to face the stiffest battle,
But their officers drive them like chickens and dogs.
Whatever is asked of them,
Dare they complain?
For example, this winter
Held west of the gate,
Challenged for taxes,
How could they pay?
. . . We have learned that to have a son is bad luck—
It is very much better to have a daughter
Who can marry and live in the house of a neighbour,
While under the sod we bury our boys.
. . . Go to the Blue Sea, look along the shore
At all the old white bones forsaken—
New ghosts are wailing there now with the old,
Loudest in the dark sky of a stormy day.

Tu Fu

A SONG OF LIANG-CHOU

They sing, they drain their cups of jade,
They strum on horseback their guitars.
. . . Why laugh when they fall asleep drunk on the sand?—
How many soldiers ever come home?

Wang Han

WAR IN CHANG-AN CITY

Chang-an in utter confusion
as though wolves and tigers had been
let loose; and I turned into a refugee
seeking to escape from my own country
to the borders of another; my home sad
and bitter that I must go; my friends wishing
to escape with me.

Leaving the city
one saw nothing, for the horror of the surroundings
blotted out all else; everywhere
the white bones of the dead were
scattered and on the roads were starving women
putting the children they could not feed
into the grass to die;
the abandoned child cries, yet the mother
dare not turn her head, though herself
shedding tears, saying she knew not where
she would die herself, and surely both
could not keep alive; and I, rather than
listen to such bitter words, goad my horse
along faster;
on the South I climb to Pa Ling, looking
back at Chang-an; then, thinking of the good king
who lies there, long with a broken heart
for the sweet day of peace.

WANG TSAN

(Translated from the Chinese by Rewi Alley)

OFFICIAL VISIT TO SHIH HAO VILLAGE

One sunset I came to Shih Hao village and
shortly there followed
an official, seizing conscripts;
in the courtyard of the peasant's home where I stayed
an old man quickly got over the wall and vanished.

To the door came his old wife to greet the official
as best she could;
he, in great anger, swore at her,
but she answered bitterly, and I heard her words:

"I have had three sons taken
to be soldiers at Yeh Cheng
then came a letter saying that two had
been killed and the third never knew
which day he would die.

Now in this hut there is
none but a baby grandson
whose mother still suckles him;
she cannot go out as she has no clothing
to cover her nakedness.

All I can do is go back with you
to the battle at Hoyang;
there I can cook, even though I am old—
take me, spare them."

Night wore on
the sound of voices died away
until there was left coming from the hut, only
the sobbing of the daughter-in-law;

at dawn I rose and left
with only the old man
to bid me good-bye.

TU FU

(Translated from the Chinese by Rewi Alley)

THE NEFARIOUS WAR

Last year we fought by the head-stream of the So-Kan,
This year we are fighting on the Tsung-ho road.
We have washed our armor in the waves of the Chiao-chi lake,
We have pastured our horses on Tien-shan's snowy slopes.
The long, long war goes on ten thousand miles from home.
Our three armies are worn and grown old.

The barbarian does man-slaughter for plowing;
On his yellow sand-plains nothing has been seen but blanched
    skulls and bones.
Where the Chin emperor built the walls against the Tartars,
There the defenders of Han are burning beacon fires.
The beacon fires burn and never go out.
There is no end to war!—

In the battlefield men grapple each other and die;
The horses of the vanquished utter lamentable cries to heaven,
While ravens and kites peck at human entrails,
Carry them up in their flight, and hang them on the branches of
    dead trees.
So, men are scattered and smeared over the desert grass,
And the generals have accomplished nothing.

Oh, nefarious war! I see why arms
Were so seldom used by the benign sovereigns.

LI PO

(Translated from the Chinese by Shigeyoshi Obata)

THE WAR YEAR

Lowland hills and rivers
    dragged on to the war map
O lowlands lowlands O!
Those groaning people!
    how can they live?
       A turnip or two
       grubbed up
Don't talk to me
    about titles
       promotions
       all that slop
One general
    pulling out a victory
       leaves
    ten
    thousand
    corpses
       to rot!

               Ts'AO SUNG

(Translated from the Chinese by
C. H. Kwock and Vincent
McHugh)

THE HOMETOWN HERO COMES HOME

This train, two Illinois counties late,
slips through jungles of corn and hot leaves,
and the blazing helmets of huge barns.

My head spins with too much beer and sun
and the mixed feelings of going home.

The coach window has melted my face.
I itch where a birthmark darkens my skin.

The Jewish woman who sits next to me
sheds tears for a son, dead in Viet Nam.
Her full lips are the color of crushed plums.
I want to go off with her to some lost
fishing village on the Mississippi
and be quiet among stones and small boats.

My fever breaks in the Galena hills.

It's too humid; no one will meet me.
And there are no brass bands in Dubuque.

DAVE ETTER

THE MOUND IN THE MEADS

This is the mound that holds the slain
Who came to the meads to fight the Dane,
Who came to the meads from hut and hall,
Fair-haired Saxons lusty and tall,
Earl and churl, and thane and thrall.

For they went not back to hut and hall:
On his golden bracelet swore the Dane
That none should be left uncleft in twain.
And this is the hillock that hides them all,
This is the mound that holds the slain.

For the Northman spared not great or small,
Him of the hut or him of the hall,
Earl or churl, or thane or thrall,
And this is the barrow that hides them all;
This is the mound that holds the slain.

WILLIAM WATSON

NERO'S TERM

Nero was not alarmed when he heard
the prophecy of the Delphic Oracle.
"Let him fear the seventy-three years."
There was still ample time to enjoy himself.
He is thirty years old. The term
the god allots to him is quite sufficient
for him to prepare for perils to come.

Now he will return to Rome slightly fatigued,
but delightfully fatigued from this journey,
which consisted entirely of days of pleasure
at the theaters, the gardens, the athletic fields . . .
evenings spent in the cities of Greece . . .
Ah the voluptuous delight of nude bodies, above all . . .

These things Nero thought. And in Spain Galba
secretly assembles and drills his army,
the old man of seventy-three.

C. P. CAVAFY

THE ROMAN ROAD

Hot and stubborn hills endure
Where Romans damned the temperature.

They grunted under *sarcinae*
And eyed the shadows longingly;

Commended Vercingetorix,
Caesar also, to the Styx;

Regretted leaving Tuscan field
To lug a javelin, pack a shield.

Doughboys now in like contrition
Sweat the eternal expedition:

Sergeant, Captain, Major, Pershing
Butts for scientific cursing.

Though we're making history
And saving poor Democracy,

All the ghosts along the road
Gesture in the soldier's code;

Nod and wink and signify
Other hopes to cheer the dry:

At the village just ahead
There'll be straw for soldier's bed

And time to nose out cautiously
Des oeufs ... du pain ... vin du pays.

DONALD DAVIDSON
1918–1919

DIDO OF TUNISIA

I had heard of these things before—of chariots rumbling
   Through desolate streets, of the battle cries and the danger,
And the flames rising up, and the walls of the houses crumbling.
   It was told to me by a stranger.

But it was for love of the fair and long-robed Helen,
  The stranger said (his name still troubles my sleep),
That they came to the windy town he used to dwell in,
  Over the wine-dark deep.

In the hollow ships they came, though the cost was dear.
  And the towers toppled, the heroes were slain without pity.
But whose white arms have beckoned these armies here
  To trample my wasted city?

Ah, this, Aeneas, you did not tell me of:
That men might struggle and fall, and not for love.

PHYLLIS McGINLEY

GRASS

Pile the bodies high at Austerlitz and Waterloo.
Shovel them under and let me work—
    I am the grass; I cover all.

And pile them high at Gettysburg
And pile them high at Ypres and Verdun.
Shovel them under and let me work.
Two years, ten years, and passengers ask the conductor:
    What place is this?
    Where are we now?

    I am the grass.
    Let me work.

CARL SANDBURG

PROLONGED SONNET

(When the Troops were returning from Milan)

If you could see, fair brother, how dead beat
    The fellows look who come through Rome to-day,—
    Black yellow smoke-dried visages,—you'd say
They thought their haste at going all too fleet.
Their empty victual-waggons up the street
    Over the bridge dreadfully sound and sway;
    Their eyes, as hanged men's, turning the wrong way;
And nothing on their backs, or heads, or feet.
One sees the ribs and all the skeletons
    Of their gaunt horses; and a sorry sight
Are the torn saddles, crammed with straw and stones.
    They are ashamed, and march throughout the night;
Stumbling, for hunger, on their marrowbones;
    Like barrels rolling, jolting, in this plight.
Their arms all gone, not even their swords are saved;
And each as silent as a man being shaved.

NICCOLO DEGLI ALBIZZI
(Translated by Dante Gabriel Rossetti)

BOOKRA

"As I lay asleep in Italy."
—Shelley

One night I lay asleep in Africa,
In a closed garden by the city gate;
A desert horseman, furious and late,
Came wildly thundering at the massive bar,

"Open in Allah's name! Wake, Mustapha!
Slain is the Sultan,—treason, war, and hate
Rage from Fez to Tetuan! Open straight."
The watchman heard as thunder from afar:
"Go to! In peace this city lies asleep;
To all-knowing Allah 't is no news you bring;"
Then turned in slumber still his watch to keep.
At once a nightingale began to sing,
In oriental calm the garden lay,—
Panic and war postponed another day.

CHARLES DUDLEY WARNER

AFTER BLENHEIM

It was a summer evening,
    Old Kaspar's work was done,
And he before his cottage door
    Was sitting in the sun;
And by him sported on the green
His little grandchild Wilhelmine.

She saw her brother Peterkin
    Roll something large and round
Which he beside the rivulet
    In playing there had found;
He came to ask what he had found
That was so large and smooth and round.

Old Kaspar took it from the boy
    Who stood expectant by;
And then the old man shook his head,
    And with a natural sigh
" 'Tis some poor fellow's skull," said he,
"Who fell in the great victory.

"I find them in the garden,
    For there's many here about,
And often when I go to plow
    The ploughshare turns them out.
For many thousand men," said he,
"Were slain in that great victory."

"Now tell us what 'twas all about,"
    Young Peterkin he cries;
And little Wilhelmine looks up
    With wonder-waiting eyes;
"Now tell us all about the war,
And what they fought each other for."

"It was the English," Kaspar cried,
    "Who put the French to rout;
But what they fought each other for
    I could not well make out.
But every body said," quoth he,
"That 'twas a famous victory.

"My father lived at Blenheim then,
    Yon little stream hard by;
They burnt his dwelling to the ground,
    And he was forced to fly;
So with his wife and child he fled,
Nor had he where to rest his head.

"With fire and sword the country round
    Was wasted far and wide,
And many a childing mother then
    And newborn baby died:
But things like that, you know, must be
At every famous victory.

"They say it was a shocking sight
    After the field was won;
For many thousand bodies here
    Lay rotting in the sun:
But things like that, you know, must be
After a famous victory.

"Great praise the Duke of Marlbro' won
  And our good Prince Eugene";
"Why 'twas a very wicked thing!"
  Said little Wilhelmine;
"Nay . . . nay . . . my little girl," quoth he,
"It was a famous victory.

"And every body praised the Duke
  Who this great fight did win."
"But what good came of it at last?"
  Quoth little Peterkin:—
"Why that I cannot tell," said he,
"But 'twas a famous victory."

ROBERT SOUTHEY

REVIEWING NEGRO TROOPS GOING
SOUTH THROUGH WASHINGTON,
APRIL 26, 1864

And while the others
On the sidewalk stared
At him for what he did,
He gravely bared
His heavy head
To the chesty Negro ranks
And gave to them
His color-blinding thanks.

PAUL HORGAN

BLACK KETTLE RAISES THE
STARS AND STRIPES

"Nits make lice," said Chivington.
"Kill the nits and you'll get no lice."

The white men burst in at sunrise, shooting and stabbing.
And there was old Black Kettle
Tying the Stars and Stripes to his tent pole,
And the squaws running in every direction

Around Sand Creek,
A swept corner of the American consciousness

And it's no use playing the tuba to a dead Indian.

LOUIS SIMPSON

THE ARSENAL AT SPRINGFIELD

This is the Arsenal. From floor to ceiling,
  Like a huge organ, rise the burnished arms;
But from their silent pipes no anthem pealing
  Startles the villages with strange alarms.

Ah! what a sound will rise, how wild and dreary,
  When the death-angel touches those swift keys!
What loud lament and dismal Miserere
  Will mingle with their awful symphonies!

I hear even now the infinite fierce chorus,
  The cries of agony, the endless groan,
Which, through the ages that have gone before us,
  In long reverberations reach our own.

On helm and harness rings the Saxon hammer,
  Through Cimbric forest roars the Norseman's song,
And loud, amid the universal clamor,
  O'er distant deserts sounds the Tartar gong.

I hear the Florentine, who from his palace
  Wheels out his battle-bell with dreadful din,
And Aztec priests upon their teocallis
  Beat the wild war-drums made of serpent's skin;

The tumult of each sacked and burning village;
  The shout that every prayer for mercy drowns;
The soldiers' revels in the midst of pillage;
  The wail of famine in beleaguered towns;

The bursting shell, the gateway wrenched asunder,
  The rattling musketry, the clashing blade;
And ever and anon, in tones of thunder
  The diapason of the cannonade.

Is it, O man, with such discordant noises,
  With such accursed instruments as these,
Thou drownest Nature's sweet and kindly voices,
  And jarrest the celestial harmonies?

Were half the power, that fills the world with terror,
  Were half the wealth bestowed on camps and courts,
Given to redeem the human mind from error,
  There were no need of arsenals or forts:

The warrior's name would be a name abhorred!
  And every nation, that should lift again
Its hand against a brother, on its forehead
  Would wear forever more the curse of Cain!

Down the dark future, through long generations,
  The echoing sounds grow fainter and then cease;
And like a bell, with solemn, sweet vibrations,
  I hear once more the voice of Christ say, "Peace!"

Peace! and no longer from its brazen portals
  The blast of War's great organ shakes the skies!
But beautiful as songs of the immortals,
  The holy melodies of love arise.

HENRY WADSWORTH LONGFELLOW

RELIEVING GUARD

Came the relief. "What, sentry, ho!
How passed the night through thy long waking?"
"Cold, cheerless, dark,—as may befit
The hour before the dawn is breaking."

"No sight? no sound?" "No; nothing save
The plover from the marshes calling,
And in yon western sky, about
An hour ago, a star was falling."

"A star? There's nothing strange in that."
"No, nothing; but, above the thicket,
Somehow it seemed to me that God
Somewhere had just relieved a picket."

BRET HARTE

TO THE WARMAKERS

Mow down the young. Trample them under your boot.
Their stalks are slim and tender, supple and green;
They will not clog the blades, they will not blunt the machine.
Weed out the young before they take firm root.

Let the young pay your debts, furnish your tolls.
With a synthetic glamour invest
Their sacrifice. They know not how to protest.
Murder their bodies. Desecrate their souls.

Let the black phoenix of evil rise on the young.
Theirs be the blunder, theirs the bloody task.
You will not be here when the future ages ask:
"Where are the hands for building? Where are the songs
   unsung?"

EDITH LOVEJOY PIERCE

D'ARTAGNAN

The road to Paris stretches broad ahead;
   From side to side great trees their shadows throw
   Across the moon-bathed path. A hidden foe
Lurks in the forest shade, mayhap, where spread
The royal oaks. The world is still and dead,
   Save for a horseman, riding hard, bent low
   Upon his horse's lathered neck, as though
On pilgrimage of life and death he sped.

D'Artagnan! Gad, the name seems to enthrall!
   Duellist, soldier, Gascon, I would give
      A year of life for just one hour's delight
With you, in court or camp or tavern brawl;
   But most—and always will the picture live—
      For one mad dash to Paris in the night.

VINCENT STARRETT

TWO FUNERALS

Upon a field of shrieking red
  A mighty general stormed and fell.
They raised him from the common dead
  And all the people mourned him well.
"Swiftly," they cried, "let honors come,
  And Glory with her deathless bays;
For him let every valiant drum
  And grieving bugle thrill with praise.
Has he not made the whole world fear
  The very lifting of his sword—
Has he not slain his thousands here
  To glorify Law and the Lord!
Then make his bed of sacred sod;
  To greater heights no man can win."
And each amused and ancient god
    Began to grin.

Facing a cold and sneering sky,
  Cold as the sneering hearts of men,
A man began to prophesy,
  To speak of love and faith again.
Boldly he spoke, and bravely dared
  The cruel word, the kindlier stone;
The armies mocked at him; he fared
  To battle gaily—and alone.
Alone he fought; alone, to move
  A world whose wars would never cease,
And all his blows were struck for love,
  And all his fighting was for peace.
They tortured him with thorns and rods,
  They hanged him on a frowning hill—
And all the old and heartless gods
    Are laughing still.

LOUIS UNTERMEYER

THE KINGS ARE PASSING DEATHWARD

The Kings are passing deathward in the dark
    Of days that had been splendid where they went;
Their crowns are captive and their courts are stark
    Of purples that are ruinous, now, and rent.
For all that they have seen disastrous things:
    The shattered pomp, the split and shaken throne,
They cannot quite forget the way of Kings:
    Gravely they pass, majestic and alone.

With thunder on their brows, their faces set
    Toward the eternal night of restless shapes,
They walk in awful splendour, regal yet,
    Wearing their crimes like rich and kingly capes. . . .
Curse them or taunt, they will not hear or see;
The Kings are passing deathward: let them be.

                            DAVID MORTON

NAPOLEON IN HADES

They stirred uneasily, drew close their capes,
    And whispered each to each in awed surprise,
Seeing this figure brood along the shapes,
    World tragedies thick-crowding through his eyes.
On either side the ghostly groups drew back
    In huddled knots, yielding him way and room,
Their foolish mouths agape and fallen slack,
    Their bloodless fingers pointing through the gloom.

Still lonely and magnificent in guilt,
    Splendid in scorn, rapt in a cloudy dream,
He paused at last upon the Stygian silt,
    And raised calm eyes above the angry stream. . . .
Hand in his breast, he stood till Charon came,
While Hades hummed with gossip of his name.

DAVID MORTON

UNTITLED SONNET

Not ours to ask why, when we are done,
The little time we spent before the sun
Was bought so dearly, with such wealth of grief,
Such wasted hopes, such sad betrayed belief.

Not ours to ask why you, who had the wealth
To waste a billion stars on empty space,
Could find but one cold world, one dying sun,
For those who might find meaning in your grace.

Not ours to ask why, of endless time
You spent on tearing galaxies apart
You gave but one short day, one bitter day
To those who have your image in their heart.
It is not we shall ask. We shall be dumb,
Back in the nothing that you drew us from.

JOSEPH SELIGMAN

THE PERSIAN VERSION

Truth-loving Persians do not dwell upon
The trivial skirmish fought near Marathon.
As for the Greek theatrical tradition
Which represents that summer's expedition
Not as a mere reconnaissance in force
By three brigades of foot and one of horse
(Their left flank covered by some obsolete
Light craft detached from the main Persian fleet)
But as a grandiose, ill-starred attempt
To conquer Greece—they treat it with contempt;
And only incidentally refute
Major Greek claims, by stressing what repute
The Persian monarch and the Persian nation
Won by this salutary demonstration:
Despite a strong defence and adverse weather
All arms combined magnificently together.

ROBERT GRAVES

BLACK DOUGLAS

He shall no more be seen.
Rejoice! Rejoice!
For his voice
Shall no more be heard,
And the lowliest bird
May strut like a queen
Over his bed.
He is dead! He is dead!

You may start in your sleep,
Night after night,
And in fright,
Hear a sound at your door;
'Twill be Douglas no more.
He lies in a heap
Of dust under clover—
His conquests are over.

He shall not re-appear.
Go to your rest.
The Moors have pressed
Him under their feet,
And the trumpets are sweet,
Proclaiming the clear
Tale of the cast—
Down terror at last.

O be fearless, be free,
Be gay and be proud,
Sing aloud!
No matter what new
Thing cuts you in two,
It will not be he.
The dust has him now,
The dust has him now!

HELENE MULLINS

LINCOLNSHIRE BOMBER STATION

Across the road the homesick Romans made
The ground-mist thickens to a milky shroud;
Through flat, damp fields call sheep, mourning their dead
In cracked and timeless voices, unutterably sad,
Suffering for all the world, in Lincolnshire.

And I wonder how the Romans liked it here;
Flat fields, no sun, the muddy misty dawn,
And always, above all, the mad rain dripping down,
Rusting sword and helmet, wetting the feet
And soaking the bone, down to the very heart. . . .

HENRY TREECE

THERMOPYLAE 1941

It is not easy to fight at Thermopylae.
You need double courage, for you are fighting
Another man's battle. Thermopylae can never
Belong to us. He was brave, the Australian
Farmer who fell there in nineteen forty-one
With an oath that lashed the rock. Every pass
Must be defended once, and Leonidas
Had made his inimitable stand.
But the gods enjoy playing soldiers, dressing them
In pretty clothes, and putting them to fight
On the same fields. Soldiers, they think, are made of lead,
And anyhow should not know where or why they fight.
But if the quality of the lead is bad
And they can feel? What then? Fight, soldier, fight.
For now that the shattered ships, the tanks and guns,
Held by the spring-flowers of the pass, look like broken
Toys of children that have grown up and gone away,
The Stranger will still go to Sparta, but he will
Announce also the death of the Australian farmer.
Leonidas is only a matter of precedence.

C. A. TRYPANIS

VETERAN

He was a brave man at Château-Thierry
And endured all things in the Argonne Wood.
And now he's drunk as an owl and bleary
And fat and feeble and no damned good.

And he's laughing hard at a fly-specked story
Whose point's in the use of that strange word bitch.
Human glory is transitory.
Yet once he was tuned up to concert pitch.

And Siegfried and Roland would not have disowned him
And the cross-grained courage that could not weary.
What is it that has discrowned and dethroned him?
He's a long, long distance from Château-Thierry.

LEONARD BACON

UNCLE FRANK

My Uncle Frank was a magnificent hater.
Forty years later he still said Lee was a traitor.
You couldn't argue with him. All said and done,
He had walked two miles under fire at Fort Donelson.

LEONARD BACON

DISASTERS OF WAR:
GOYA AT THE MUSEUM

Streets opening like wounds: Madrid's. The thresh
Of resistance ends before a tumbled wall;
    The coward and the cursing sprawl
    Brotherly, one white heap of flesh
    Char-mouthed and boneyard black.
A woman, dragged off, howls—a lively sack
Of loot. An infant, fallen on its back,
Scowls from the stones at the Herodian lark.
Light is the monster fattening on this dark.

If shadow takes cadavers for her chair,
Where fresh fires glare life lifts a wolfish snout.
    Bruised and abused by hope, the rout,
    Turning, is gunned across the square
    And scattered. Rope, knife, lead
Slice prayer short. A lolling head
Grins, as with toothache. Stubbornly, the dead
Thrust forward like a beggar's senseless claw.
What is scrawled there in acid? THIS I SAW.

Beyond the Madonnas and marbles, Goya's brute
Testament pits itself against the hush
    Of the blond halls, the urbane crush—
    Against the slat-eyed, the astute,
    Craning, against the guard, who yawns.
And pits itself in vain: this dark, these dawns,
Vomit of an old war, things the nightmare spawns
Are pictures at an exhibition. We
Look, having viewed too much, and cannot see.

BABETTE DEUTSCH

EPITAPH FOR A LEADER

They stood abreast in the meadow,
Between dusk and dark,
In the last hour, the sweet final air;
And the youngest cried out—
"Mother! Mother!"
As the firing squads took aim.
They were buried in mass graves.

But you, Franco, when you come to die?
Bishops and archbishops will kneel by your bed,
You will have a state funeral,
And the procession will never be over.

It will wind and wend its way
Through history, the narrow defiles
Of text and exegesis,
Bronze data and marble facts—   ,
Whom you brought in to help you,
And what the term is for such acts.
It is the same term everywhere.

Turbaned Moors on white horses
Will brandish lances no more,
Or guard your memory
As they guarded you.

CHARLES NORMAN

THE MOORS FIGHT ON THE SIDE OF GOD

The Moors fight on the side of God,
   They do His will in Spain;
The roads they took are lonely now,
   And haunted by the slain.

O little children with the dead,
   Who will not taller grow,
The last road home was dark and long,
   Because God willed it so.

CHARLES NORMAN

THE BENEDICTION:
An Incident of the Spanish Civil War

> "The Pope gave his apostolic benediction
> to a group of Spanish generals from
> Madrid."
>
> A.P. dispatch, 1939
>
> *"Et Dominus ait: Cain, Cain,*
> *Ubi Abel? Abel, frater tuus?"*

i

Behold the Bishop of Rome:
A saint man and a sage.

He speaketh to urb and orb. The generals
Are blessed. The sword is blessed.

Wrapped in white wool, anointed with the oil,
The lion Victory becomes the Lamb.

His voice shall rise among the praising choirs.
Here in the tolling twilight of the west,

Blessing, the Bishop of Rome
Lays, for a healing unction, balm and oil

On bombed Guernica and on Badajoz.

ii
Here is another twilight, and the same:
A pock of earth, a breach of broken stones

And silence, shaken only where
Speaking to urb and orb

A voice goes seeking, calling:
"Cain, Cain, Cain! Where is your brother Abel?

"Abel your brother—where is Abel, Cain?"
In bombed Guernica and in Badajoz

Calling among the ruins of those stones.

MAURICE ENGLISH

FASCIST LIMERICKS

On the height of the proud Campidoglio
They are cheering the General Badoglio.
He has won in the field,
But they can't clean their shield
With Gold Dust, or Lux, or Sapolio.

All losers curse those who are winning.
Eels, of course, have objections to skinning.
But every dictator
Will sooner or later
Find the thing he thought finished beginning.

LEONARD BACON

"NO QUARREL"

"We have no quarrel with the German nation"—
   One would not quarrel with the trustful sheep:
But generation after generation
   They cough up rulers who disturb our sleep.

"We have no quarrel with the German nation."
   They're fond of music, poetry, and beer:
But, all the same, with tiresome iteration
   They choose a fool to govern them—and cheer.

"We have no quarrel with the German nation";
   But no one else upsets the common pot.
They are the cause of every conflagration—
   Is it a mere coincidence, or what?

We had no quarrel with the German nation
   When Wilhelm was the madman off the chain;
We helped along their rehabilitation—
   And now, my hat, they do it all again!

"We have no quarrel with the German nation";
   And Wagner's works are very good indeed:
But if they *must* repeat this aberration
   It might be better if they did not breed.

"We have no quarrel with the German nation";
  In their affairs of course we have no say:
But it would seem some major operation
  (On head and heart) may be the only way.

                A. P. HERBERT
              September 20, 1939

PORTRAIT OF A SENATOR

The senator said,
Adjusting the waistcoat of his mind
Inside his leonine head:

"Americans are not going to fight
Because of some mistreated Jews
In Europe." He was right.

America went to war
For Frenchmen, Danes and Dutch,
For Poles and Czechs, for—

Glory be to God—
The peoples of the earth.
The senator must have thought it odd;

And having all he desired,
The statesman's mantle, money in the bank,
Thereupon retired.

The earth spun like a top,
Himself its center, which was pleasant,
Even though he could not make it stop.

Town hall and country house
Knew him; but if ideas were cheese,
He could not have caught a mouse,

Under the table his expanding gut
Expanded; the ample chair
Graciously received his butt.

Beyond the rim of his plate
Trudged the disinherited.
Ipse dixit, 1938.

CHARLES NORMAN

FRANCE

I hate to think that pompous men in spurs
    Are swilling claret where we used to dine,
And Mademoiselle, with that sad smile of hers,
    Is wasting on the Hun her wit and wine.

One thought alone can comfort me at night,
    When I recall the *Café de la Lune:*
If what the temperance fellows say is right
    He'll have cirrhosis of the liver soon.

A. P. HERBERT

August 4, 1940

ON THE EYES OF AN SS OFFICER

I think of Amundsen, enormously bit
By arch-dark flurries on the ice plateaus,
An amorist of violent virgin snows
At the cold end of the world's spit.

Or a Bombay saint asquat in the market place,
Eyes gone from staring the sun over the sky,
Who still dead-reckons that acetylene eye
An eclipsed mind in a blind face.

But this one's iced or ashen eyes devise,
Foul purities, in flesh their wilderness,
Their fire; I ask my makeshift God of this
My opulent bric-a-brac world to damn his eyes.

RICHARD WILBUR

"AND THEN THERE WERE NONE"

Ten white ptarmigan
    Perching in a pine;
Hitler gave his solemn oath:
    And then there were nine.

Nine white ptarmigan
    Trusting in their fate;
Hitler gave his solemn oath:
    And then there were eight.

Eight white ptarmigan
  Putting trust in Heaven;
Hitler gave his solemn oath:
  And then there were seven.

Seven white ptarmigan
  In a pretty fix;
Hitler gave his solemn oath:
  And then there were six.

Six white ptarmigan
  Hoping to survive;
Hitler gave his solemn oath:
  And then there were five.

Five white ptarmigan
  Wishing they were more;
Hitler gave his solemn oath:
  And then there were four.

Four white ptarmigan
  Trying to agree;
Hitler gave his solemn oath:
  And then there were three.

Three white ptarmigan
  Feeling very few;
Hitler gave his solemn oath:
  And then there were two.

Two white ptarmigan
  Cried, "It can't be done!"
Hitler gave his solemn oath:
  And then there was one.

One white ptarmigan
  Looked about and blinked;
Hitler gave his solemn oath:
  The race is now extinct.

EDNA ST. VINCENT MILLAY

ONLY THE BEARDS ARE DIFFERENT

Among the first to go are always a few
Of the strong man's friends, crumpling up
Against the sun-pocked wall, relieved at last
Of the terrible burden of his friendship.
Cruel necessity follows him everywhere.
And the face that was once a dream
Of a patch of baked earth to the landless
And a living wage has lost its inner light,
Faded, and now, deathless and untrue,
Flaps in the memory like a wind-blown poster.
Behind the monolithic smile, the frighteningly
Public eyes, a thousand trigger-fingers tense;
Sadist and pimp resume
Their tricky trades. Caught in two minds,
Men look the other way when truth cries out, that leprous
Mendicant whose importunity must be discouraged.
Travellers find the once-welcoming
Doors closed to them now; over the evening meal
The children are eyed suspiciously, radios
Turned up louder and louder to cover
All the embarrassing noises a revolution makes
In passing—the tumbrils, the firing-squads, the screams
From the underground prison,
The rifle-butts at the door, the conspirators' whisper,
The drums, the marching-songs, the hysterical spiel
Of bandaleroed barkers plugging the ancient wares....

Somewhere the country's saviour cries in his sleep.

BRUCE DAWE

CZECHO-SLOVAKIA

If there were balm in Gilead, I would go
To Gilead for your wounds, unhappy land,
Gather you balsam there, and with this hand,
Made deft by pity, cleanse and bind and sew
And drench with healing, that your strength might grow,
(Though love be outlawed, kindness contraband)
And you, O proud and felled, again might stand;
But where to look for balm, I do not know.
The oils and herbs of mercy are so few;
Honour's for sale; allegiance has its price;
The barking of a fox has bought us all;
We save our skins a craven hour or two.—
While Peter warms him in the servants' hall
The thorns are platted and the cock crows twice.

EDNA ST. VINCENT MILLAY

PROLOGUE

Born to flying glass
bombs   strafing   shrapnel   murder
from me   expect no pleasing tones
no obscurities
Reared in the light of the fires
gorging themselves on human flesh
my mind was clarified.

Kind words   I was not born to
but the shout to shelter fast
To trees   or to birds   I was not born
nor to a king of any kind

nor to ambiguity
I was born to people   in distress
held captive   celebrating death

I was born to hate
and the bible for my life
was in the propaganda books
Enemy   nazi   jackboot
—the words that thrilled me first
Flames that light my life
to flying glass born

Keith Barnes

FOOTNOTE

It was an age of invention—
The sealed van, guaranteed,
Everyone dead on arrival;
Made in Germany.

All frontiers wore
The latest in landscapes,
Proliferous wire
Over vanished woods.

Nearly everyone lived
In the exile's country,
And nobody knows
Where the birds went.

Our wars were chiefly
Waged against children,
Perpetual trudgers
On endless newsreels.

Charles Norman

WITHOUT BENEFIT OF DECLARATION

Listen here, Joe
Don't you know
That tomorrow
You got to go
Out yonder where
The steel winds blow?

Listen here, kid,
It's been said
Tomorrow you'll be dead
Out there where
The snow is lead.

Don't ask me why.
Just go ahead and die.
Hidden from the sky
Out yonder you'll lie;
A medal to your family—
In exchange for
A guy.

Mama, don't cry.

LANGSTON HUGHES

DRAFT NOTICE

They ignored my name and I was a number
—less than a dried leaf in a herbarium.
Their hands plucked my number, gelidly, zealously;
on a post card they wrote it, unperturbed.

Invitation to die ... but for what?
Invitation to kill ... but for whom?
Oh shadowy secretary, precipitate
hurried executioner, hidden
behind a rapid illegible squiggle,
what will you say of my name and of others,
what will you say about me and about others,
on the Day of Judgment, impending, imminent
—what will you say if your hand did not quiver
as it rapidly scribbled that squiggle?

I know that your hand is only the instrument
but beyond your shoulder you belong to you.
You might well have wept, have hesitated ...
—A tearstain would suffice
to give meaning to our death
convoked by your indifference!

DAVID MOURÃO-FERREIRA

TO CERTAIN LADIES, ON GOING
TO THE WARS

Goodbye ladies, O ladies sweet, goodbye,
No more the gentle flowers,
Another life I'll try.
No more the scented evenings,
The tussels in the hay,
It's time that I was leaving
To live another way.

O, there'll be blood, my ladies
(And not all mine, I hope),
And damp beds under hedges
And washing without soap.

Black lice will bite the body
That knew your friendly limbs;
In barrack-blocks I'll envy
Your silken-sheeted rooms.

But goodbye ladies, O ladies don't complain,
It's time I learnt to shoot straight
Or fly an aeroplane.
So many lads I knew once
Are rotting under sods;
I owe them this one journey—
So farewell, pretty bird.

HENRY TREECE

REFLECTIONS UPON A RECURRENT SUGGESTION BY CIVIL DEFENSE AUTHORITIES THAT I BUILD A BOMBSHELTER IN MY BACKYARD

I remember a dug-out we dug in the backyard as children
And closed on top with an old door covered with dirt
And sat in hour by hour, thoroughly squashed
But safe, with our chins on our knees, from the world's hurt.
There, as the earth trickled down on us as in an hour glass,
Our mothers called us, called us to come and be fed,
But we would not, could not hear them, possessed as we were
By our self's damp stronghold among the selfless dead.

This and a few other fantasies of my youth
I remember now as scenes in a marathon play
That plunged on for act after act with the lost hero
Preferring, to death, some brave kind of decay.
While he was still on stage I grew up
And sneaked away as he battered his hemlock cup.

Now, they say, willy-nilly I must go back,
And under the new and terrible rules of romance
Dig yet another hole in which like a child
My adult soul may trifle with circumstance.
But I'll not, no, not do it, not go back
And lie there in that dark under the weight
Of all that earth on that old door for my state.
I know too much to think now that, if I creep
From the grown-up's house to the child's house, I'll keep.

REED WHITTEMORE

PATTERN

She was there before Caesar's day
And she is still there,
The woman at the doorway, watching.
The man walks off, self-conscious in his new clothes;
He turns around once and tries to grin.
She is not quite sure about his saving the nation,
Or the empire, or freedom, or the world.
Sowing seeds, pitching hay—ah yes, he was good at that·
The wind blows, and prying fingers of rain
Meddle with the listless autumn leaves.
The woman turns to face the familiar room
That has died during the last five minutes.
Life narrows into a thin cold draft of loneliness,
Even while she fondles the little boy,
Quiet and awed at her side.
The late rose on the kitchen table drops its petals one by one.

EDITH LOVEJOY PIERCE

RUINS

Where a bomb fell
The wall is sheared away.
A bathroom pipe leads nowhere.
Around the fireplace on the third floor
Invisible ghosts sit in the air
Extending foggy hands
Toward a cold grate.

There is no roof on the bombed church.
The walls are broken.
But not a tombstone is cracked:
The dead were left in peace.
White lilies grow out of the handclasp
Of the new dead and the old.

After ten years
The ruins have acquired
The smoothness of age.
It is too late now to rebuild.
Telescoped through time
These empty shells of houses
Have joined the Roman relics
In a patina of the past.

EDITH LOVEJOY PIERCE

A BOY

Out of the noise of tired people working,
    Harried with thoughts of war and lists of dead,
His beauty met me like a fresh wind blowing,
    Clean boyish beauty and high-held head.

Eyes that told secrets, lips that would not tell them,
  Fearless and shy the young unwearied eyes—
Men die by millions now, because God blunders,
  Yet to have made this boy he must be wise.

SARA TEASDALE

THERE ARE NO GOOD GIANTS

Once more the strong reach out. The weapons vary:
gold, gun . . . a missionary.
But the force is there, the force is always there,

the force of steel or an editorial . . . tribal, economic force,
topographical.
The persuasion of bread, as irresistible as knife held to the
throat—
of dialectics, as convincing as God . . . or an atom bomb.

Once more the historic words, the slogans . . . the familiar
names that have bloodied man's record.
Oil. Dardanelles. Balance of power. Outlet to the sea.

The strong reach out in all directions, there are no good
giants . . . O believe this—
correct the fables, revise your children's nursery rhymes,
tell them it is wrong even for the good to be too strong.

Even a lover turns tyrant . . . with love's scepter for power.

WALTER BENTON

WHAT WERE THEY LIKE?

1) Did the people of Viet Nam
   use lanterns of stone?
2) Did they hold ceremonies
   to reverence the opening of buds?
3) Were they inclined to quiet laughter?
4) Did they use bone and ivory,
   jade and silver, for ornament?
5) Had they an epic poem?
6) Did they distinguish between speech and singing?

1) Sir, their light hearts turned to stone,
   It is not remembered whether in gardens
   stone lanterns illumined pleasant ways.
2) Perhaps they gathered once to delight in blossom,
   but after the children were killed
   there were no more buds.
3) Sir, laughter is bitter to the burned mouth.
4) A dream ago, perhaps. Ornament is for joy.
   All the bones were charred.
5) It is not remembered. Remember,
   most were peasants; their life
   was in rice and bamboo.
   When peaceful clouds were reflected in the paddies
   and the water buffalo stepped surely along terraces,
   maybe fathers told their sons old tales.
   When bombs smashed those mirrors
   there was time only to scream.
6) There is no echo yet
   of their speech which was like a song.
   It was reported their singing resembled
   the flight of moths in moonlight.
   Who can say? It is silent now.

DENISE LEVERTOV

SPEECH BY MOONLIGHT

Listen, I love you:
The Germans are marching;
The moon's at the full:
Look, they are flying;
By moonlight, in silver,
The old cities slumbered;
Now the silver cities
Are dying, dying.

What shall I tell you?
Great beauty is passing:
The Germans are up—
The Germans are flying;
The silver cities
Turn gold and ruby;
The old cities
Are dying.

CHARLES NORMAN

ON A PORTRAIT BY COPLEY

The General requires a portrait;
Copley is at length engaged
to represent, with art and passion,
Mars, the bellicose, enraged.

His countenance, conflagratory,
speaks of fire, and smoke, and war.
His gaze, he says, goes forward with
"That freedom I have foughten for."

So let his eye be falcon-sharp—
let every grizzly sinew tense
into the rigid pose. "I say
attack! The *devil* with defense!"

And for effect, a cannon at
the canvas border. "War is Hell . . ."
A flag to furl above him. "Yet,
I served my country long and well."

Is *Copley* taken in? Not quite.
We see a ruddy windbag, whose
combustious face and eyes are bright
with apoplexy, bulk, and booze.

ARTHUR FREEMAN

DEATH AND GENERAL PUTNAM

His iron arm has spent its force,
No longer might he rein a horse;
Lone, beside the dying blaze
Dreaming dreams of younger days
  Sat old Israel Putnam.

Twice he heard, then three times more
A knock upon the oaken door,
A knock he could not fail to know,
That old man in the ember-glow.
  "Come," said General Putnam.

The door swung wide; in cloak and hood
Lean and tall the pilgrim stood
And spoke in tones none else might hear,
"Once more I come to bring you Fear!"
  "Fear?" said General Putnam.

"You know not Fear? And yet this face
Your eyes have seen in many a place
Since first in stony Pomfret, when
You dragged the mad wolf from her den."
        "Yes," said General Putnam.

"Was I not close, when, stripped and bound
With blazing fagots heaped around
You heard the Huron war cry shrill?
Was I not close at Bunker Hill?"
        "Close," said General Putnam.

"Am I not that which strong men dread
On stricken field or fevered bed
On gloomy trail and stormy sea,
And dare you name my name to me?"
        "Death," said General Putnam.

"We have been comrades, you and I,
In chase and war beneath this sky;
And now, whatever Fate may send,
Old comrade, can you call me friend?"
        "Friend!" said General Putnam.

Then up he rose, and forth they went
Away from battleground, fortress, tent,
Mountain, wilderness, field and farm,
Death and the General, arm-in-arm,
        Death and General Putnam.

                          ARTHUR GUITERMAN

EPITAPH ON A JACOBITE

To my free king I offered free from stain
Courage and faith: vain faith, and courage vain.
For him, I threw lands, honors, wealth, away,
And one dear hope, that was more prized than they.

For him I languished in a foreign clime,
Gray-haired with sorrow in my manhood's prime;
Heard on Lavernia Scargill's whispering trees,
And pined by Arno for my lovelier Tees;
Beheld each night my home in fevered sleep,
Each morning started from the dream to weep;
Till God, who saw me tried too sorely, gave
The resting-place I asked, an early grave.
O thou, whom chance leads to this nameless stone,
From that proud country which was once mine own,
By those white cliffs I never more must see,
By that dear language which I spake like thee,
Forget all feuds, and shed one English tear
O'er English dust. A broken heart lies here.

Thomas Babington, Lord Macaulay

✵ ✵

THE SOLDIER ✓

If I should die, think only this of me:
  That there's some corner of a foreign field
That is for ever England. There shall be
  In that rich earth a richer dust concealed;
A dust whom England bore, shaped, made aware,
  Gave, once, her flowers to love, her ways to roam,
A body of England's, breathing English air,
  Washed by the rivers, blest by suns of home.

And think, this heart, all evil shed away,
  A pulse in the eternal mind, no less
    Gives somewhere back the thoughts by England given;
Her sights and sounds; dreams happy as her day;
  And laughter, learnt of friends; and gentleness,
    In hearts at peace, under an English heaven.

Rupert Brooke

✵ ✵

I HAVE A RENDEZVOUS WITH DEATH

I have a rendezvous with Death
At some disputed barricade,
When Spring comes back with rustling shade
And apple-blossoms fill the air—
I have a rendezvous with Death
When Spring brings back blue days and fair.

It may be he shall take my hand
And lead me into his dark land
And close my eyes and quench my breath—
It may be I shall pass him still.
I have a rendezvous with Death
On some scarred slope of battered hill,
When Spring comes round again this year
And the first meadow-flowers appear.

God knows 'twere better to be deep
Pillowed in silk and scented down,
Where love throbs out in blissful sleep,
Pulse nigh to pulse, and breath to breath,
Where hushed awakenings are dear . . .
But I've a rendezvous with Death
At midnight in some flaming town,
When Spring trips north again this year,
And I to my pledged word am true,
I shall not fail that rendezvous.

ALAN SEEGER

BEETHOVEN'S NINTH SYMPHONY
IN WARTIME

This music is entrusted to the heart of man:
It cannot be unmade, lost or forgotten.
No bursting bomb can flatten out this resonance
Or mutilate these rhythms.
This is a strong resilient bridge
With one abutment
Mortised in Beethoven's mind,
The other firmly braced
Against a far-off world of brotherhood,
A bright gold cliff of joy.
Here is an arch where human souls
Pass dry-shod above the torrent
Of scarlet savagery that floods our age.

EDITH LOVEJOY PIERCE

MUSIC ROOM

Filling the northern embrasure, the grand.
The violin case propped to the wall.
Half open beside it the music stand.
The windows are solemn and tall
And covered with patterns of lace like a swirl of frost.
The tones of the music are lost.

To this quiet, white enclosure nobody comes.
Yet threads from this center are spun
As far as the western moon, as far as the eastern sun.
There, in a corner, the drums.

The days and the months go by. Spring will come back.
Spring only—half sensed and not understood.
The empty ash tray, the unpolished wood.
"Ah, Dream of Love" left on the music rack.
Far off, the sound of guns, the sight of burning wings.
The music asleep in the strings.

EDITH LOVEJOY PIERCE

SOLDIER ASLEEP

Soldier asleep, and stirring in your sleep,
In tent, trench, dugout, foxhole, or swampy slough,
I pray the Lord your rifle and soul to keep,
And your body, too,

From the hid sniper in the leafy tangle,
From shrapnel, from the barbed and merciless wire,
From tank, from bomb, from the booby trap in the jungle,
From water, from fire.

It was an evil wind that blew you hither,
Soldier, to this strange bed—
A tempest brewed from the world's malignant weather.

Safe may you sleep, instead,
Once more in the room with the pennants tacked on the wall,
Or the room in the bachelor apartment, 17 L,
The club room, the furnished room across the hall,
The room in the cheap hotel,

The double-decker at home, the bench in the park,
The attic cot, the hammock under the willow,
Or the wide bed in the remembered dark
With the belovèd's head beside you on the pillow.

Safe may the winds return you to the place
That, howsoever it was, was better than this.

PHYLLIS McGINLEY

Soldiers who wish to be a hero
Are practically zero,
But those wishing to be civilians,
Jesus, they run into the millions.

Anonymous GI, World War II
(*Scribbled on latrine wall in England*)

THE SEND-OFF

Down the close, darkening lanes they sang their way
To the siding-shed,
And lined the train with faces grimly gay.

Their breasts were stuck all white with wreath and spray
As men's are, dead.

Dull porters watched them, and a casual tramp
Stood staring hard,
Sorry to miss them from the upland camp.
Then, unmoved, signals nodded, and a lamp
Winked to the guard.

So secretly, like wrongs hushed-up, they went.
They were not ours:
We never heard to which front these were sent.

Nor there if yet they mock what women meant
Who gave them flowers.

Shall they return to beating of great bells
In wild train-loads?
A few, a few, too few for drums and yells,
May creep back, silent, to still village wells
Up half-known roads.

WILFRED OWEN

NAMING OF PARTS

Today we have naming of parts. Yesterday,
We had daily cleaning. And tomorrow morning,
We shall have what to do after firing. But today,
Today we have naming of parts. Japonica
Glistens like coral in all of the neighbouring gardens,
    And today we have naming of parts.

This is the lower sling swivel. And this
Is the upper sling swivel, whose use you will see,
When you are given your slings. And this is the piling swivel,
Which in your case you have not got. The branches
Hold in the gardens their silent, eloquent gestures,
    Which in our case we have not got.

This is the safety-catch, which is always released
With an easy flick of the thumb. And please do not let me
See anyone using his finger. You can do it quite easy
If you have any strength in your thumb. The blossoms
Are fragile and motionless, never letting anyone see
    Any of them using their finger.

And this you can see is the bolt. The purpose of this
Is to open the breech, as you see. We can slide it
Rapidly backwards and forwards; we call this
Easing the spring. And rapidly backwards and forwards
The early bees are assaulting and fumbling the flowers:
　　They call it easing the Spring.

They call it easing the Spring. It is perfectly easy
If you have any strength in your thumb: like the bolt,
And the breech, and the cocking-piece, and the point of balance,
Which in our case we have not got; and the almond-blossom
Silent in all of the gardens and the bees going backwards and
　　forwards,
　　For today we have naming of parts.

HENRY REED

THE SERGEANT MAJOR

　　This curse on legs,
　　An ill-wind blowing in the Square,
　　The regrettable sharp outcry coming therefrom,
　　This is the Sergeant Major.

　　His spindle shanks incredibly support
　　A pendulous belly perilously belted.

　　With pointed teeth that drip,
　　Dear God I have seen him smile.

　　He lives in a world of as-you-were,
　　Circumscribed with shun.

　　I do not feel
　　That I shall come to love
　　The Sergeant Major.

KENNETH HOPKINS

GUNNERY PRACTICE

It is always there, rattling the teacups at four,
Tilting the seagull on his favorite perch,
Twitting his gaudy eye. But in the town,
Well used to it, bread is delivered as usual.

Casual week-enders and furlough brides express
A barbed impatience at its thoughtlessness
And snap a flower's neck or steal a kiss
To scatter the dark shock with countershock.

Shaking the smooth midsummery ocean,
Invisible convulsions mumble in space
Like answering Jehovah. For one wide moment
The ragged flags of panic skitter in the air.

Carefully, though, the embarrassed gull rearranges
His feathers and his nerves, the maiden aunt
With valor pours five cups, and the soldier's girl
In the soldier's hat races to the bandstand.

Fondly the mellowing sun comes down, tracing
The shoreline with its burning pencils, tipping
The lightly balanced shell; and what,
In other times, was privilege for love

Of seascapes or girls is shadow and suspicion.
The evenings are private with but a little laughter;
Songs on a sea-warped piano, perhaps, will sound
Between the soft topple and recess of waves,

Giving sentiment a small identity
While slow tides like unanswered questions withdraw,
And the time is unresolved in the quietude of guns,
And the lights go down like suns drowned in the sea.

JOHN MALCOLM BRINNIN

THE ARTICLES OF WAR

Do I forget the Articles of War?
Herded into a bare mess hall
We stood against the unaccommodating wall
Or squatted on the floor
To hear what they could hang or shoot us for.

All of us green, but one greener by half,
Green enough to stand out in the crowd,
Asked (since questions were allowed)
"Can you resign from the Army?" The laugh
We gave him! How we hooted at the calf!

Hootable, I suppose, was Henry Thoreau
Whose equally unaccommodating fate
It was to try to disentangle from the State.
But Liberty would not let him go.
The State said: "Henry, no."

Somebody next, who knows? may try
Resigning from the human race,
Somebody aghast at history,
Haunted by hawk's eyes in the human face.
Somebody—could it be I?

ROBERT FRANCIS

THE LAST DAY OF LEAVE

(1916)

We five looked out over the moor
At rough hills blurred with haze, and a still sea:
Our tragic day, bountiful from the first.

We would spend it by the lily lake
(High in a fold beyond the farthest ridge),
Followed the cart-track till it faded out.

The time of berries and bell-heather;
Yet all that morning nobody went by
But shepherds and one old man carting turfs.

We were in love: he with her, she with him,
And I, the youngest one, the odd man out,
As deep in love with a yet nameless muse.

No cloud; larks and heath-butterflies,
And herons undisturbed fishing the streams;
A slow cool breeze that hardly stirred the grass.

When we hurried down the rocky slope,
A flock of ewes galloping off in terror,
There shone the waterlilies, yellow and white.

Deep water and a shelving bank.
Off went our clothes and in we went, all five,
Diving like trout between the lily groves.

The basket had been nobly filled:
Wine and fresh rolls, chicken and pineapple—
Our braggadocio under threat of war.

The fire on which we boiled our kettle
We fed with ling and rotten blackthorn root;
And the coffee tasted memorably of peat.

Two of us might stray off together
But never less than three kept by the fire,
Focus of our uncertain destinies.

We spoke little, our minds in tune—
A sigh or laugh would settle any theme;
The sun so hot it made the rocks quiver.

But when it rolled down level with us,
Four pairs of eyes sought mine as if appealing
For a blind-fate-aversive afterword:—

"Do you remember the lily lake?
We were all there, all five of us in love,
Not one yet killed, widowed or broken-hearted."

ROBERT GRAVES

MISERICORDIA

He earned his bread by making wooden soldiers,
With beautiful golden instruments,
Riding dapple-grey horses.
But when he heard the fanfare of trumpets
And the long rattle of drums
As the army marched out of the city
He took all his soldiers
And burned them in the grate;
And that night he fashioned a ballet-dancer
Out of tinted tissue-paper,
And the next day he started to carve a Pietà
On the steel hilt
Of a cavalry sword.

AMY LOWELL

ANTHEM FOR DOOMED YOUTH

What passing-bells for these who die as cattle?
    Only the monstrous anger of the guns.
    Only the stuttering rifles' rapid rattle
Can patter out their hasty orisons.

No mockeries now for them; no prayers nor bells,
    Nor any voice of mourning save the choirs,—
The shrill, demented choirs of wailing shells;
    And bugles calling for them from sad shires.

What candles may be held to speed them all?
    Not in the hands of boys, but in their eyes
Shall shine the holy glimmers of good-bys.
    The pallor of girls' brows shall be their pall;
Their flowers the tenderness of patient minds,
And each slow dusk a drawing-down of blinds.

WILFRED OWEN

THE SPIRES OF OXFORD

I saw the spires of Oxford
    As I was passing by,
The gray spires of Oxford
    Against the pearl-gray sky.
My heart was with the Oxford men
    Who went abroad to die.

The years go fast in Oxford,
    The golden years and gay,
The hoary Colleges look down
    On careless boys at play.
But when the bugles sounded war
    They put their games away.

They left the peaceful river
    The cricket-field, the quad,
The shaven lawns of Oxford,
    To seek a bloody sod—
They gave their merry youth away
    For country and for God.

God rest you, happy gentlemen,
  Who laid your good lives down,
Who took the khaki and the gun
  Instead of cap and gown.
God bring you to a fairer place
  Than even Oxford town.

WINIFRED M. LETTS

"THERE WILL COME SOFT RAINS"
(War Time)

There will come soft rains and the smell of the ground,
And swallows circling with their shimmering sound;

And frogs in the pools singing at night,
And wild plum-trees in tremulous white;

Robins will wear their feathery fire
Whistling their whims on a low fence-wire;

And not one will know of the war, not one
Will care at last when it is done.

Not one would mind, neither bird nor tree
If mankind perished utterly;

And Spring herself, when she woke at dawn,
Would scarcely know that we were gone.

SARA TEASDALE

PASTORAL

Village, empty now, and laid in ruin,
Who will raise your walls against the rain?
Pasture, where the sheep were wont to wander,
Will the shepherd ever come again?

Wood, poor blackened wood where passed the battle,
How should bough of yours again be green?
Field—oh, plowed and sown indeed, but barren,
Long the reaper waits, and waits in vain.

PAUL SCOTT MOWRER
Aisne

SPRING MCMXL

London Bridge is falling down, Rome's burnt, and Babylon
The Great is now but dust; and still Spring must
Swing back through Time's continual arc to earth.
Though every land become as a black field
Dunged with the dead, drenched by the dying's blood,
Still must a punctual goddess waken and ascend
The rocky stairs, up into earth's chilled air,
And pass upon her mission through those carrion ranks,
Picking her way among a maze of broken brick
To quicken with her footsteps the short sooty grass between;
While now once more their futile matchwood empires flare and
    blaze
And through the smoke men gaze with bloodshot eyes
At the translucent apparition, clad in trembling nascent green,
Of one they can still recognize, though hardly understand.

DAVID GASCOYNE

FLOWERS AT HAMPTON COURT

The chestnut trees in Bushey Park are lit
 This year as always since the spring knows naught
Of war and death, and still the shadows flit
 Across the dappled grass and burnish it.
And still at night the moon is stately sort
 Is tranquil with the avenues, and lights
 The sleeping palace, as on other nights
 Of springs long past; but searching for the rose
 In vain, the dawn a little whisper knows:
"Where are the flowers that were at Hampton Court?"

Two years ago when all the trees were green
 The old red walls were unto the summer brought,
By joyous band of lilies and the lean
 Daffodils danced before or ran between.
Where are they gone these blooms of good report?
 And where the lad and where the laughing maid
 Who came to wonder and to love who stayed?
 For a lost flower is a little thing
 But a lost lover is the end of spring.
"Where are the flowers that were at Hampton Court?"

Ah! spring these flowers are growing otherwhere,
 In a new soil a changing radiance taught,
Born of the soul and nourished of the air,
 Sweeter though scentless and unseen more fair.
Where are they gone these blooms of good report?
 Is it perhaps that where the Tigris flows
 There blooms an unaccustomed English rose?
 And where the guns have killed the spring in France
 The English lilies break a silver lance?
"Where are the flowers that were at Hampton Court?"

If thus the flowers, where are those who here
   Themselves fresh flowers with the springtime fraught,
Saw the first leaves in Bushey Park appear
The dead swept leaves the leaves of yesteryear?
   Where are they gone those lads of good report?
   It may be they are sleeping; it may be
   Strange lands have taken them or a strange sea.
   But wheresoever in the world they lie
   An English voice till that world ends will cry
"Here are the flowers that were at Hampton Court!"

                      HUMBERT WOLFE

FRANCE

Today you'll find by field and ditch
The small invasion of the vetch:
And where they sleep rest-harrow will
Follow upon the daffodil.

These in their soft disordered ranks
Withstand and overcome the Tanks;
And the small unconsidered grass
Cries to the gunner "On ne passe."

The corn outlasts the bayonet,
Whose blades no blood nor rest can fret,
Or only the immortal rust
Of poppies failing in their thrust.

The lines these hold no force can break,
Nor their platoons advancing shake,
Whose wide offensive wave on wave
Doth make a garden of a grave.

These with the singing lark conspire
To veil with loveliness the wire,
While he ascending cleans the stain
In heaven of the aeroplane.

These in the fields and open sky
Reverse the errors of Versailles,
Who with a natural increase
From year to year establish peace.

For all the living these will cloak
The things they spoiled, the hearts they broke;
And where these heal the earth will be
For all the dead indemnity.

HUMBERT WOLFE

IN THE THIRD YEAR OF WAR

I dream now of green places,
And the gentle kine
Wading knee-deep in rushes;

I dream of singing birds,
And summer rain,
And gracious, homely words.

But I wake to bitter winds,
And blown sand's whine
Across forgotten lands;

And empty skies at night,
And cold star-shine
Where lonely spirits meet.

I feel all this, my dear,
Alone, my love, alone
With all the old fear.

I dream now there is no ending,
No golden, breathless dawn;
Only seeking, seeking without finding.

HENRY TREECE

MY SWEET OLD ETCETERA

my sweet old etcetera
aunt lucy during the recent

war could and what
is more did tell you just
what everybody was fighting

for,
my sister

isabel created hundreds
(and
hundreds) of socks not to
mention shirts fleaproof earwarmers

etcetera wristers etcetera, my
mother hoped that

i would die etcetera
bravely of course my father used
to become hoarse talking about how it was
a privilege and if only he
could meanwhile my

self etcetera lay quietly
in the deep mud et

cetera
(dreaming
et
    cetera, of
Your smile
eyes knees and of your Etcetera)

E. E. CUMMINGS

THE TRUMPET

O how after Arcturus
have you and your companions
heard the laughter and the distant shout
of this long tube a man sets to his mouth
crying that war is sweet, and the men you
see asleep after fighting will fight in the day before us?

Since with manual skill
men dressed to kill in purple
with how many strange tongues
cried the trumpet, that cried once
for the death of Hector from Troy steeple
that cried when a hundred hopes fell.

Tonight we heard it
who for weeks have only listened
to the howls of inhuman voices.
But, as the apprehensive ear rejoiced
breathing the notes in, the sky glistened
with a flight of bullets. We must be up early

tomorrow, to forget the cry and the crier
as we forgot the conversation
of our friends killed last month, last week
and hear, crouching, the air shriek
the crescendo, expectancy to elation
violently arriving. The trumpet is a liar.

KEITH DOUGLAS
Middle East R.A.C. Base Depot

V.D.F.

(Ave atque Vale)

You from Givenchy, since no years can harden
    The beautiful dead, when holy twilight reaches
    The sleeping cedar and the copper beeches
Return to walk again in Wadham Garden.
We, growing old, grow stranger to the College,
    Symbol of youth, where we were young together,
    But you, beyond the reach of time and weather,
Of youth in death forever keep the knowledge.
We hoard our youth, we hoard our youth and fear it,
    But you, who freely gave what we have hoarded,
    Are with the final goal of youth rewarded
The road to travel and the traveller's spirit.
And, therefore, when for us the stars go down,
Your star is steady over Oxford Town.

HUMBERT WOLFE

FOR CARLOS, AT WAR

Look well, Carlos, look for two
There in that strange continent half a world away.
Gather all strange beauty into store,
All strange music and dreams on people's faces.
Gather all hates and ugliness, too. I shall want to know
How the mountains rose and how the waters fell,
How it was with you those nights and days
When pain was and when peace was with you.
   Look well, Carlos. I shall keep count, too,
Of these familiar things: how the seasons went
Strewing their splendid colors on this land;
How dawn burned in brilliant colors each new light;
How the cardinal, red comet in a snow-caught bush,
Sang on Christmas Eve.
   Such beauty burned you to happiness
Long years ago when peace was more than dream.
Some far and golden day we'll meet together.
Hand will renew its knowledge of another hand.
That room which you remember will be light and warm,
And there we'll spread our hearts' packs on the floor,
Each searching for treasure in the other's pack.
And all things in your company will be treasured lore.
   Look well, Carlos. I shall look for you.

MERLE PRICE

WAR SONG

Soldier, in a curious land
  All across a swaying sea,
Take her smile and lift her hand—
  Have no guilt of me.

Soldier, when were soldiers true?
　　If she's kind and sweet and gay,
Use the wish I send to you—
　　Lie not lone till day!

Only, for the nights that were,
　　Soldier, and the dawns that came,
When in sleep you turn to her
　　Call her by my name.

DOROTHY PARKER

1944

THE GENERAL

"Good-morning; good-morning!" the General said
When we met him last week on our way to the line.
Now the soldiers he smiled at are most of 'em dead,
And we're cursing his staff for incompetent swine.
"He's a cheery old card," grunted Harry to Jack
As they slogged up to Arras with rifle and pack.

*   *   *

But he did for them both by his plan of attack.

SIEGFRIED SASSOON

BASE DETAILS

If I were fierce, and bald, and short of breath,
　　I'd live with scarlet Majors at the Base,
And speed glum heroes up the line to death.
　　You'd see me with my puffy petulant face,

Guzzling and gulping in the best hotel,
  Reading the Roll of Honour. "Poor young chap,"
I'd say—"I used to know his father well;
  Yes, we've lost heavily in this last scrap."
And when the war is done and youth stone dead,
I'd toddle safely home and die—in bed.

SIEGFRIED SASSOON

A LETTER FROM THE FRONT

I was out early today, spying about
From the top of a haystack—such a lovely morning—
And when I mounted again to canter back
I saw across a field in the broad sunlight
A young Gunner Subaltern, stalking along
With a rook-rifle held at the ready, and—would you believe
    it?—
A domestic cat, soberly marching beside him.

So I laughed, and felt quite well disposed to the youngster,
And shouted out "the top of the morning" to him,
And wished him "Good sport!"—and then I remembered
My rank, and his, and what I ought to be doing:
And I rode nearer, and added, "I can only suppose
You have not seen the Commander-in-Chief's order
Forbidding English officers to annoy their Allies
By hunting and shooting."
                    But he stood and saluted
And said earnestly, "I beg your pardon, Sir,
I was only going out to shoot a sparrow
To feed my cat with."
                    So there was the whole picture,
The lovely early morning, the occasional shell

Screeching and scattering past us, the empty landscape,—
Empty, except for the young Gunner saluting,
And the cat, anxiously watching his every movement.

I may be wrong, and I may have told it badly,
But it struck *me* as being extremely ludicrous.

HENRY NEWBOLT

VERGISSMEINICHT

Three weeks gone and the combatants gone,
returning over the nightmare ground
we found the place again, and found
the soldier sprawling in the sun.

The frowning barrel of his gun
overshadowing. As we came on
that day, he hit my tank with one
like the entry of a demon.

Look. Here in the gunpit spoil
the dishonoured picture of his girl
who has put: *Steffi. Vergissmeinicht*
in a copybook gothic script.

We see him almost with content
abased, and seeming to have paid
and mocked at by his own equipment
that's hard and good when he's decayed.

But she would weep to see today
how on his skin the swart flies move;
the dust upon the paper eye
and the burst stomach like a cave.

For here the lover and killer are mingled
who had one body and one heart.
And death who had the soldier singled
has done the lover mortal hurt.

KEITH DOUGLAS
Homs, Tripolitania, 1943

ELEGY JUST IN CASE

Here lie Ciardi's pearly bones
In their ripe organic mess.
Jungle blown, his chromosomes
Breed to a new address.

Here lies the sgt.'s mortal wreck
Lily spiked and termite kissed,
Spiders pendant from his neck
And a beetle on his wrist.

Bring the tic and southern flies
Where the land crabs run unmourning
Through a night of jungle skies
To a climeless morning.

And bring the chalked eraser here
Fresh from rubbing out his name.
Burn the crew-board for a bier.
(Also Colonel what's-his-name.)

Let no dice be stored and still
Let no poker deck be torn.
But pour the smuggled rye until
The barracks threshold is outworn.

File the papers, pack the clothes,
Send the coded word through air—
"We regret and no one knows
Where the sgt. goes from here."

JOHN CIARDI

JOHN ANDERSON

John Anderson, a scholarly gentleman
advancing with his company in the attack
received some bullets through him as he ran.

So his creative brain whirled, and he fell back
in the bloody dust (it was a fine day there
and warm). Blood turned his tunic black

while past his final desperate stare
the other simple soldiers run
and leave the hero unaware.

Apt epitaph or pun
he could not hit upon, to grace
a scholar's death; he only eyed the sun.

But I think, the last moment of his gaze
beheld the father of gods and men,
Zeus, leaning from heaven as he dies,

whom in his swoon he hears again
summon Apollo in the Homeric tongue:
Descend Phoebus and cleanse the stain

of dark blood from the body of John Anderson.
Give him to Death and Sleep,
who'll bear him as they can

out of range of darts to the broad vale
of Lycia; there lay him in a deep
solemn content on some bright dale.

And the brothers, Sleep and Death
lift up John Anderson at his last breath.

KEITH DOUGLAS
Oxford, 1940

DREAMERS

Soldiers are citizens of death's gray land,
   Drawing no dividend from time's tomorrows.
In the great hour of destiny they stand,
   Each with his feuds, and jealousies, and sorrows.
Soldiers are sworn to action; they must win
   Some flaming, fatal climax with their lives.
Soldiers are dreamers; when the guns begin
   They think of firelit homes, clean beds, and wives.

I see them in foul dug-outs, gnawed by rats,
   And in the ruined trenches, lashed with rain,
Dreaming of things they did with balls and bats,
   And mocked by hopeless longing to regain
Bank-holidays, and picture shows, and spats,
   And going to the office in the train.

SIEGFRIED SASSOON

AT CARNOY

Down in the hollow there's the whole Brigade
Camped in four groups: through twilight falling slow
I hear a sound of mouth-organs, ill-played,
And murmur of voices, gruff, confused, and low.
Crouched among thistle-tufts I've watched the glow
Of a blurred orange sunset flare and fade;
And I'm content. To-morrow we must go
To take some cursèd Wood . . . O world God made!

SIEGFRIED SASSOON
July 3rd, 1916

THE BATTLE

Helmet and rifle, pack and overcoat
Marched through a forest. Somewhere up ahead
Guns thudded. Like the circle of a throat
The night on every side was turning red.

They halted and they dug. They sank like moles
Into the clammy earth between the trees.
And soon the sentries, standing in their holes,
Felt the first snow. Their feet began to freeze.

At dawn the first shell landed with a crack.
Then shells and bullets swept the icy woods.
This lasted many days. The snow was black.
The corpses stiffened in their scarlet hoods.

Most clearly of that battle I remember
The tiredness in eyes, how hands looked thin
Around a cigarette, and the bright ember
Would pulse with all the life there was within.

LOUIS SIMPSON

STRANGE MEETING

It seemed that out of battle I escaped
Down some profound dull tunnel, long since scooped
Through granites which Titanic wars had groined.
Yet also there encumbered sleepers groaned,
Too fast in thought or death to be bestirred.
Then, as I probed them, one sprang up, and stared
With piteous recognition in fixed eyes,
Lifting distressful hands as if to bless.
And by his smile, I knew that sullen hall,
By his dead smile I knew we stood in Hell.
With a thousand pains that vision's face was grained;
Yet no blood reached there from the upper ground,
And no guns thumped, or down the flues made moan.
"Strange friend," I said, "here is no cause to mourn."
"None," said that other, "save the undone years,
The hopelessness. Whatever hope is yours,
Was my life also; I went hunting wild
After the wildest beauty in the world,
Which lies not calm in eyes, or braided hair,
But mocks the steady running of the hour,
And if it grieves, grieves richlier than here.
For of my glee might many men have laughed,
And of my weeping something had been left,
Which must die now. I mean the truth untold,
The pity of war, the pity war distilled.

Now men will go content with what we spoiled,
Or, discontent, boil bloody, and be spilled.
They will be swift with swiftness of the tigress,
None will break ranks, though nations trek from progress.
Courage was mine, and I had mystery,
Wisdom was mine, and I had mastery:
To miss the march of this retreating world
Into vain citadels that are not walled.
Then, when much blood had clogged their chariot-wheels,
I would go up and wash them from sweet wells,
Even with truths that lie too deep for taint.
I would have poured my spirit without stint
But not through wounds; not on the cess of war.
Foreheads of men have bled where no wounds were.
I am the enemy you killed, my friend.
I knew you in this dark; for so you frowned
Yesterday through me as you jabbed and killed.
I parried; but my hands were loath and cold.
Let us sleep now. . . ."

WILFRED OWEN

PINNED DOWN

I was in the dust,
With every breath I drank it,
And burrowed as I must
Into the earth to thank it

For keeping me concealed
Below the roof of lead
That flew across the field
Close above my head.

I got there by a blunder,
I awaited a command,
But only my heart's thunder
Sounded in the land.

Would I lie there forever?
When might I rise and run?
Never, never, never,
When they blew out the sun.

PAUL HORGAN

COUNTER-ATTACK

We'd gained our first objective hours before
While dawn broke like a face with blinking eyes,
Pallid, unshaved and thirsty, blind with smoke.
Things seemed all right at first. We held their line,
With bombers posted, Lewis guns well placed,
And clink of shovels deepening the shallow trench.
  The place was rotten with dead; green clumsy legs
  High-booted, sprawled and grovelled along the saps;
  And trunks, face downward, in the sucking mud,
  Wallowed like trodden sand-bags loosely filled;
  And naked sodden buttocks, mats of hair,
  Bulged, clotted heads slept in the plastering slime.
  And then the rain began,—the jolly old rain!

A yawning soldier knelt against the bank,
Staring across the morning blear with fog;
He wondered when the Allemands would get busy;
And then, of course, they started with five-nines
Traversing, sure as fate, and never a dud.
Mute in the clamour of shells he watched them burst
Spouting dark earth and wire with gusts from hell,

While posturing giants dissolved in drifts of smoke.
He crouched and flinched, dizzy with galloping fear,
Sick for escape,—loathing the strangled horror
And butchered, frantic gestures of the dead.

An officer came blundering down the trench:
"Stand-to and man the fire-step!" On he went . . .
Gasping and bawling, "Fire-step . . . counter-attack!"
   Then the haze lifted. Bombing on the right
   Down the old sap: machine-guns on the left;
   And stumbling figures looming out in front.
   "O Christ, they're coming at us!" Bullets spat,
And he remembered his rifle . . . rapid fire . . .
And started blazing wildly . . . then a bang
Crumpled and spun him sideways, knocked him out
To grunt and wriggle: none heeded him; he choked
And fought the flapping veils of smothering gloom,
Lost in a blurred confusion of yells and groans . . .
Down, and down, and down, he sank and drowned,
Bleeding to death. The counter-attack had failed.

SIEGFRIED SASSOON

THE BLOODY SIRE

It is not bad. Let them play.
Let the guns bark and the bombing-plane
Speak his prodigious blasphemies.
It is not bad, it is high time,
Stark violence is still the sire of all the world's values.

What but the wolf's tooth chiseled so fine
The fleet limbs of the antelope?
What but fear winged the birds and hunger
Gemmed with such eyes the great goshawk's head?
Violence has been the sire of all the world's values.

Who would remember Helen's face
Lacking the terrible halo of spears?

Who formed Christ but Herod and Caesar,
The cruel and bloody victories of Caesar?
Violence has been the sire of all the world's values.

Never weep, let them play,
Old violence is not too old to beget new values.

ROBINSON JEFFERS

THE EFFECT

"The effect of our bombardment was terrific. One man told me he had never seen so many dead before."
—War Correspondent.

"He'd never seen so many dead before."
They sprawled in yellow daylight while he swore
And gasped and lugged his everlasting load
Of bombs along what once had been a road.
"How peaceful are the dead."
Who put that silly gag in some one's head?

"He'd never seen so many dead before."
The lilting words danced up and down his brain,
While corpses jumped and capered in the rain.
No, no; he wouldn't count them any more . . .
The dead have done with pain;
They've choked; they can't come back to life again.

When Dick was killed last week he looked like that,
Flapping along the fire-step like a fish,
After the blazing crump had knocked him flat . . .
*"How many dead? As many as you wish.
Don't count 'em; they're too many.
Who'll buy my nice fresh corpses, two a penny?"*

SIEGFRIED SASSOON

BEFORE THE CHARGE

(*Loos, 1915*)

The night is still and the air is keen,
Tense with menace the time crawls by,
In front is the town and its homes are seen,
Blurred in outline against the sky.

The dead leaves float in the sighing air,
The darkness moves like a curtain drawn,
A veil which the morning sun will tear
From the face of death. We charge at dawn.

PATRICK MacGILL

THE DAY OF BATTLE

"Far I hear the bugle blow
To call me where I would not go,
And the guns begin the song,
'Soldier, fly or stay for long.'

"Comrade, if to turn and fly
Made a soldier never die,
Fly I would, for who would not?
'Tis sure no pleasure to be shot.

"But since the man that runs away
Lives to die another day,
And cowards' funerals, when they come,
Are not wept so well at home,

"Therefore, though the best is bad,
Stand and do the best, my lad;
Stand and fight and see your slain,
And take the bullet in your brain."

A. E. Housman

COMMUNIQUÉ FROM AN ARMY DESERTER PROBABLY ITALIAN

Now it's so quiet I can hear a dog
Driving his sheep through the dry valley
Out of sight. I look ahead and back.
There's nothing on the road. I obey
The order of trees.
Look how the sea deserted, pulled out.
Left stray implements, a rabble
Of lizards and snails to mock its majesty.
I salute the snail. Just for a moment
I'd like to be a school of fish leaping
After nothing. But the senators
And generals won't let me. They talk of war:
The end of the world, as if it were theirs.
They've already crippled the fields. Let the living
And the dead beware any government
Or church headed by sexless men,—just one
Can pull us all into his rancid sheets.

I call for deserters.

Stanley Moss

THE HEROES

I dreamed of war-heroes, of wounded war-heroes
With just enough of their charms shot away
To make them more handsome. The women moved nearer
To touch their brave wounds and their hair streaked with gray.

I saw them in long ranks ascending the gang-planks;
The girls with the doughnuts were cheerful and gay.
They minded their manners and muttered their thanks;
The Chaplain advised them to watch and to pray.

They shipped these rapscallions, these sea-sick battalions
To a patriotic and picturesque spot;
They gave them new bibles and marksmen's medallions,
Compasses, maps, and committed the lot.

A fine dust has settled on all that scrap metal.
The heroes were packaged and sent home in parts
To pluck at a poppy and sew on a petal
And count the long night by the stroke of their hearts.

LOUIS SIMPSON

ESCAPE

(August 6, 1916. Officer Previously Reported Died of Wounds,
Now Reported Wounded: Graves, Capt. R.,
Royal Welsh Fusiliers)

... But I *was* dead, an hour or more:
I woke when I'd already passed the door
That Cerberus guards and half-way down the road
To Lethe, as an old Greek sign-post showed.

Above me, on my stretcher swinging by,
I saw new stars in the sub-terrene sky,
A Cross, a Rose in Bloom, a Cage with Bars,
And a barbed Arrow feathered with fine stars.
I felt the vapors of forgetfulness
Float in my nostrils: Oh, may Heaven bless
Dear Lady Proserpine, who saw me wake
And, stooping over me, for Henna's sake
Cleared my poor buzzing head and sent me back
Breathless, with leaping heart along the track.
After me roared and clattered angry hosts
Of demons, heroes, and policemen-ghosts.
"Life, life! I can't be dead, I won't be dead:
Damned if I'll die for anyone," I said. . . .
Cerberus stands and grins above me now,
Wearing three heads, lion and lynx and sow.
"Quick, a revolver! but my Wedbley's gone,
Stolen . . . no bombs . . . no knife . . . (the crowd swarms on,
Bellows, hurls stones) . . . not even a honeyed sop . . .
Nothing . . . Good Cerberus . . . Good dog . . . But stop!
Stay! . . . A great luminous thought . . . I do believe
There's still some morphia that I bought on leave."
Then swiftly Cerberus' wide mouths I cram
With Army biscuit smeared with Tickler's jam;
And Sleep lurks in the luscious plum and apple.
He crunches, swallows, stiffens, seems to grapple
With the all-powerful poppy . . . then a snore,
A crash; the beast blocks up the corridor
With monstrous hairy carcase, red and dun—
Too late: for I've sped through.

O Life! O Sun!

ROBERT GRAVES

IN THE AMBULANCE

Two rows of cabbages,
Two of curly-greens,
Two rows of early peas,
Two of kidney-beans.

That's what he keeps muttering,
Making such a song,
Keeping other chaps awake
The whole night long.

Both his legs are shot away,
And his head is light,
So he keeps on muttering
All the blessed night:

Two rows of cabbages,
Two of curly-greens,
Two rows of early peas,
Two of kidney-beans.

WILFRID GIBSON

THE LAST LAUGH

"O Jesus Christ! I'm hit," he said; and died.
Whether he vainly cursed, or prayed indeed,
The Bullets chirped—In vain! vain! vain!
Machine-guns chuckled,—Tut-tut! Tut-tut!
And the Big Gun guffawed.

Another sighed,—"O Mother, mother! Dad!"
Then smiled, at nothing, childlike, being dead.
    And the lofty Shrapnel-cloud
    Leisurely gestured,—Fool!
    And the falling splinters tittered.

"My Love!" one moaned. Love-languid seemed his mood,
Till, slowly lowered, his whole face kissed the mud.
    And the Bayonets' long teeth grinned;
    Rabbles of Shells hooted and groaned;
    And the gas hissed.

WILFRED OWEN

plato told

plato told

him:he couldn't
believe it (jesus

told him;he
wouldn't believe
it) lao

tsze
certainly told
him, and general
(yes

mam)
sherman;
and even
(believe it
or

not) you
told him: i told
him; we told him
(he didn't believe it,no

sir)it took
a nipponized bit of
the old sixth

avenue
el;in the top of his head:to tell

him

E. E. CUMMINGS

BEACH BURIAL

Softly and humbly to the Gulf of Arabs
The convoys of dead sailors come;
At night they sway and wander in the waters far under,
But morning rolls them in the foam.

Between the sob and clubbing of the gunfire
Someone, it seems, has time for this,
To pluck them from the shallows and bury them in burrows
And tread the sand upon their nakedness;

And each cross, the driven stake of tidewood,
Bears the last signature of men,
Written with such perplexity, with such bewildered pity,
The words choke as they begin—

"Unknown seaman"—the ghostly pencil
Wavers and fades, the purple drips,
The breath of the wet season has washed their inscriptions
As blue as drowned men's lips,

Dead seamen, gone in search of the same landfall,
Whether as enemies they fought,
Or fought with us, or neither; the sand joins them together,
Enlisted on the other front.

El Alamein

KENNETH SLESSOR

TRENCH POETS

I knew a man, he was my chum,
But he grew blacker every day,
And would not brush the flies away,
Nor blanch however fierce the hum
Of passing shells. I used to read,
To rouse him, random things from Donne,
Like "Get with child a mandrake-root,"
But you can tell he was far gone,
For he lay gaping, mackerel-eyed,
And stiff and senseless as a post,
Even when that old poet cried,
"I long to talk with some old lover's ghost."

I tried the Elegies one day;
But he, because he heard me say,
"What needst thou have more covering than a man?"
Grinned nastily, and so I knew
The worms had got his brains at last.
There was one thing that I might do
To starve the worms; I racked my head
For healthy things and quoted *Maud*.
His grin got worse, and I could see
He laughed at passion's purity.

He stank so badly, though we were great chums
I had to leave him; then rats ate his thumbs.

EDGELL RICKWORD

DULCE ET DECORUM EST

Bent double, like old beggars under sacks,
Knock-kneed, coughing like hags, we cursed through sludge,
Till on the haunting flares we turned our backs
And towards our distant rest began to trudge.
Men marched asleep. Many had lost their boots
But limped on, blood-shod. All went lame; all blind;
Drunk with fatigue; deaf even to the hoots
Of tired, outstripped Five-Nines that dropped behind.

Gas! Gas! Quick, boys!—An ecstasy of fumbling,
Fitting the clumsy helmets just in time,
But someone still was yelling out and stumbling
And flound'ring like a man in fire or lime . . .
Dim through the misty panes and thick green light,
As under a green sea, I saw him drowning.

In all my dreams, before my helpless sight,
He plunges at me, guttering, choking, drowning.

If in some smothering dreams you too could pace
Behind the wagon that we flung him in,
And watch the white eyes writhing in his face,
His hanging face, like a devil's sick of sin;
If you could hear, at every jolt, the blood
Come gargling from the froth-corrupted lungs
Obscene as cancer, bitter as the cud
Of vile, incurable sores on innocent tongues,—
My friend, you would not tell with such high zest
To children ardent for some desperate glory,
The old lie: *Dulce et decorum est
Pro patria mori.*[1]

WILFRED OWEN

[1] "It is sweet and dignified to die for one's country."

NEWSREEL IN WARTIME
(Flame-thrower Attacking Dugout)

The red persuasion of the flames
Poured in on him and he came out
From his blind dungeon, routed by
A furnace coughing in his face.
His eyes held neither hope nor fear,
But swam in animal surprise;
He grew a coat of boiling hair
Before our eyes.
                    A popcorn sack
Split wide and crashed. A seat sighed down
Upon its hinge. The usher's light
Surprised the dark where boys-with-girls
Kissed, murmuring.
                    He slowly burned
And burning crawled and crawling died.

The scream was censored. What was left
Were less lugubrious events:
A close-up of Mount Erebus,
And babies kissing presidents.

ADRIEN STOUTENBURG

THE BAYONET
(1914)

The great guns slay from a league away, the deathbolts fly
    unseen,
And bellowing hill replies to hill, machine to brute machine,
But still in the end when the long lines bend and the battle
    hangs in doubt

They take to the steel in the same old way that their fathers
  fought it out—
It is man to man and breast to breast and eye to bloodshot eye
And the reach and twist of the thrusting wrist, as it was in the
  days gone by!

Along the shaken hills the guns their drumming thunder roll—
But the keen blades thrill with the lust to kill that leaps from
  the slayer's soul!
For hand and heart and living steel, one pulse of hate they feel.
Is your clan afraid of the naked blade? Does it flinch from the
  bitter steel?
Perish your dreams of conquest then, your swollen hopes and
  bold,
For empire dwells with the stabbing blade, as it did in the days
  of old!

DON MARQUIS

THE DEATH OF THE BALL TURRET GUNNER

From my mother's sleep I fell into the State,
And I hunched in its belly till my wet fur froze.
Six miles from earth, loosed from its dream of life,
I woke to black flak and the nightmare fighters.
When I died they washed me out of the turret with a hose.

RANDALL JARRELL

ON A VERY YOUNG, VERY DEAD SOLDIER

Where a thoughtless bullet hit his head
A keyhole bares the dark room of a dance
After the dancers, eternal until twelve,
Went down a dimming corridor and out.

What one might pay to see in operation
Merely is a color and a stuff
That bears no evidence of having been
Spectacular beyond all other gifts.

And yet, this is the brain which, after all,
Registered the burns and reared the loves
Of his short history, was dumb as clay
To bluets and to wrens but had the genius

To know the English that could turn a ball
Away from bats or into pins, knew cars
From top to bottom, sideways, inside-out,
But never queried how the planets ran.

It wired to him the pleasures he kept private
Of scaling ice across the crusted snow
When wind and moonlight gave him speed and aim;
Of swimming under water all alone.

It held the borders of the vague, round world
Down to his county's sweet geography
Of hairpin curves, long stretches of concrete
And hills his Ford ascended in high gear.

Worry of wounds that stopped to gossip here
Spoke of almost nothing but his pimples.
War was Wake and Iwo, screened of pain:
It flickered while he kissed, awaited cartoons.

Where thoughts an hour ago drummed on the heart,
Wires to the speechless tongue are strung in vain,
With neither curse nor low and awful whistle
To level at the sudden shift of things.

Life nearest to him now is creeping through
The zombi-bodied, bullet-tracking bugs,
Whose brains are warming with their pure intent
To make delicious homes behind his eyes.

O, but how he would be laughing now,
Tickled by God knows what, to see them coming,
Grim as Frankensteins: the curious look
Of conquerors on their silly, silly faces.

RICHARD GILLMAN

❋   ❋

"VALE" FROM CARTHAGE
(*Spring, 1944*)

I, now, at Carthage. He, shot dead at Rome.
Shipmates last May. "And what if one of us,"
I asked last May, in fun, in gentleness,
"Wears doom, like dungarees, and doesn't know?"
He laughed, "*Not see Times Square again?*" The foam,
Feathering across that deck a year ago,
Swept those five words—like seeds—beyond the seas
    Into his future. There they grew like trees;
    And as he passed them there next spring, they laid
    Upon his road of fire their sudden shade.
Though he had always scraped his mess-kit pure
And scrubbed redeemingly his barracks floor,
Though all his buttons glowed their ritual hymn
Like cloudless moons to intercede for him,
No furlough fluttered from the sky. He will
Not see Times Square—he will not see—he will

Not see Times
        change; at Carthage (while my friend,
Living those words at Rome, screamed in the end)
I saw an ancient Roman's tomb and read
"*Vale*" in stone. Here two wars mix their dead:
        Roman, my shipmate's dream walks hand in hand
        With yours tonight ("New York again" and "Rome"),
        Like widowed sisters bearing water home
        On tired heads through hot Tunisian sand
        In good cool urns, and says, "I understand."
Roman, you'll see your Forum Square no more;
What's left but this to say of any war?

PETER VIERECK

ON THE GRAVE OF A YOUNG CAVALRY OFFICER KILLED IN THE VALLEY OF VIRGINIA

Beauty and youth, with manners sweet, and friends—
    Gold, yet a mind not unenriched had he
Whom here low violets veil from eyes.
    But all these gifts transcended be:
His happier fortune in this mound you see.

HERMAN MELVILLE

COMMANDER DEATH

Around the cot
of a dying soldier
they have set a standing screen
in Death's honor.
Behind the screen

Commander Death
is waiting
for his dear one.
No one knows
when he will give the order
to go with him.
The mosquito curtains
along the rows
of hospital beds
seem to hover
like patches of mist.
All down the ward
the other wounded
and the sick
and the hopeful
turn their backs
upon the screen.
They play
games of cards,
tell riddles,
read letters aloud,
one softly drums on a banjo.
Lest Death
be a contagion
the patients
exaggerate
their trivial acts of life.

PAUL HORGAN

BREAKFAST

We ate our breakfast lying on our backs
Because the shells were screeching overhead.
I bet a rasher to a loaf of bread
That Hull United would beat Halifax

When Jimmy Stainthorpe played full-back instead
Of Billy Bradford. Ginger raised his head
And cursed, and took the bet, and dropt back dead.
We ate our breakfast lying on our backs
Because the shells were screeching overhead.

WILFRID GIBSON

THE JOKE

He'd even have his joke
While we were sitting tight,
And so he needs must poke
His silly head in sight
To whisper some new jest,
Chortling, but as he spoke
A rifle cracked . . .
And now God knows when I shall hear the rest.

WILFRID GIBSON

DICK MILBURN

He stood against the trunk to light his pipe
And, glancing at the green boughs overhead,
We'll pinch those almonds when they're ripe, he said.

But, now the almond-shells are brown and ripe,
Somewhere in No-man's-land he's lying dead,
And other lads are pinching them instead.

I've half a mind to save him one or two
In case his ghost comes back to claim a few,
And do the other things he meant to do.

WILFRID GIBSON

PHILIP DAGG

It pricked like needles slashed into his face,
The unceasing rustling smother of dry snow
That stormed the ridge on that hell-raking blast—

And then he knew the end had come at last,
And stumbled blindly, muttering *Cheerio!*
Into eternity, and left no trace.

WILFRID GIBSON

THE UNKNOWN SOLDIER

After a round of madness and a vague
moment of pain ... after forty winks of death, night came—

after a shuddering interval of dark, when a great hand
fell on the switch,
shorted the circuit, cut all the wires, blew out the main fuse.

And I was dredged out of the Rapido or the Rhine,
the Neckar, the Moselle,
recovered from debris of Anzio or Aachen ... Bastogne, St. Lo—
face leveled, dogtags blown off.

Charred past recognition in a gas-drenched tank.
Assembled in a shelter-half on the mined reef off Iwo Jima.
Went down. Failed to return.
Was reported lost.
Was entered missing in the morning report.

A body in the image of God was lying on the plain,
the maggot and the bluebottle cast dice for it
and black bald birds swung lower and lower for their cut.

Angels came out of their caves and lay on the ledges
sunning themselves . . . like old men or lepers—

And in the last world, quarrelsome old men
convened in domed halls and bannered parliaments to vote
for a vast, splendid, residential tomb.

WALTER BENTON

XXXVII

I did not lose my heart in summer's even
    When roses to the moonrise burst apart:
When plumes were under heel and lead was flying,
    In blood and smoke and flame I lost my heart.

I lost it to a soldier and a foeman,
    A chap that did not kill me, but he tried;
That took the sabre straight and took it striking,
    And laughed and kissed his hand to me and died.

A. E. HOUSMAN

THE MAN HE KILLED

"Had he and I but met
    By some old ancient inn,
We should have sat us down to wet
    Right many a nipperkin!

"But ranged as infantry,
    And staring face to face,
I shot at him as he at me,
    And killed him in his place.

"I shot him dead because—
Because he was my foe,
Just so: my foe of course he was;
That's clear enough; although

"He thought he'd 'list, perhaps,
Off-hand-like—just as I—
Was out of work—had sold his traps—
No other reason why.

"Yes; quaint and curious war is!
You shoot a fellow down
You'd treat, if met where any bar is,
Or help to half-a-crown."

THOMAS HARDY

WAR POEM

Don't stand at night by the gate, love,
He will not come again,
And there are eyes that laugh to see
The flowering of a pain.

Do not lay him a place, dear,
For you will eat alone;
Nor put you on that pretty dress,
The need for that is gone.

Just go into your room, lass,
And make yourself a prayer,
For that will be your strength now,
This many and many a year.

HENRY TREECE

SIC TRANSIT GLORIA

Spring shall come back, but they shall not return—
No easy resurrection split their grave,
No chalice-light redeem the funeral urn
Of those the circling seasons can not save.
The unremitting flowers of the field
Shall bead their golden laughter in the grass,
But whom the veil of death has now concealed
Shall never through the unmown meadow pass.
These fugitives no wind-borne rumor tells
Which way the fortunes of the battle went;
They see no flags, they hear no victor bells
In their far otherworldly banishment.
Some day the earth may once again be fair.
Peace may return. But they shall not be there.

EDITH LOVEJOY PIERCE

FOR LOVER MAN, AND ALL THE OTHER YOUNG MEN WHO FAILED TO RETURN FROM WORLD WAR II

Like so many other young men in those troubled
years, you abandoned your youth and your identity;
and you left the corners, the women, and the jazz
behind; and you reluctantly exchanged your three

button roll for a drab without class; then you
hurried to catch the last set at Minton's.
Bird was there and you wondered if he knew exactly
what he was trying to do; then you left—without a

kiss for Billie—for a place you had never heard of
nor ever cared existed; and there you lived with
more danger than you had ever encountered in the city.

Like so many of the young men in those troubled years,
you went away; and like so many of them you never came
back. And like so many other young hearts, Billie
was singing:

> *Oh lover man*
> *Oh where can you be?*

MANCE WILLIAMS

THE INVESTITURE

God with a Roll of Honour in His hand
Sits welcoming the heroes who have died,
While sorrowing angels ranked on either side
Stand easy in Elysium's meadow-land. '
Then *you* come shyly through the garden gate,
Wearing a blood-soaked bandage on your head;
And God says something kind because you're dead,
And homesick, discontented with your fate.

If I were there we'd snowball Death with skulls;
Or ride away to hunt in Devil's Wood
With ghosts of puppies that we walked of old.
But you're alone; and solitude annuls
Our earthly jokes; and strangely wise and good
You roam forlorn along the streets of gold.

SIEGFRIED SASSOON

TO ANY DEAD OFFICER

Well, how are things in Heaven? I wish you'd say,
    Because I'd like to know that you're all right.
Tell me, have you found everlasting day,
    Or been sucked in by everlasting night?
For when I shut my eyes your face shows pain;
    I hear you make some cheery old remark—
I can rebuild you in my brain,
    Though you've gone out patrolling in the dark.

You hated tours of trenches; you were proud
    Of nothing more than having good years to spend;
Longed to get home and join the careless crowd
    Of chaps who work in peace with Time for friend.
That's all washed out now. You're beyond the wire:
    No earthly chance can send you crawling back;
You've finished with machine-gun fire—
    Knocked over in a hopeless dud-attack.

Somehow I always thought you'd get done in,
    Because you were so desperate keen to live:
You were all out to try and save your skin,
    Well knowing how much the world had got to give.
You joked at shells and talked the usual "shop,"
    Stuck to your dirty job and did it fine:
With "Jesus Christ! when *will* it stop?
    Three years ... It's hell unless we break their line."

So when they told me you'd been left for dead
    I wouldn't believe them, feeling it *must* be true.
Next week the bloody Roll of Honour said
    "Wounded and missing"—(That's the thing to do
When lads are left in shell-holes dying slow,
    With nothing but blank sky and wounds that ache,
Moaning for water till they know
    It's night, and then it's not worth while to wake!)

* * *

Good-bye, old lad! Remember me to God,
  And tell Him that our Politicians swear
They won't give in till Prussian Rule's been trod
  Under the Heel of England ... Are you there? ...
Yes ... and the War won't end for at least two years;
But we've got stacks of men ... I'm blind with tears,
  Staring into the dark. Cheero!
I wish they'd killed you in a decent show.

SIEGFRIED SASSOON

✸   ✸

A SURVIVOR

He, not content that death had passed him by
Upon live fingers counted his dead friends
And in his shallow hole restless did lie;
They do not sleep the best who do not die
And it is not for them the battle ends.

KENNETH HOPKINS

✸   ✸

ON THE DEATH OF A MURDERER

"One day Vera showed us a photograph of some local Gestapo men which had come into her hands. The photograph had been taken when they were in the country outside Prague for a day's holiday. The young men were ranged in two rows in their neat uniforms, and they stared out at us with professionally menacing but unhappy eyes from that recent past now dead.

"... After the relief of Prague these young men were hunted through the countryside, Vera told us, like wild game, and all of them taken and killed."

Edwin Muir, *Autobiography*.

Over the hill the city lights leap up.
But here in the fields the quiet dusk folds down.
A man lies in a ditch. He listens hard.
His own fast breathing is the biggest sound,
But through it, coming nearer, he hears another:
The voices of his hunters, coming nearer.

They are coming, and he can run no further.

He was born in a Germany thrashing like a fish
On a gravel towpath beating out its life.
As a child, something they called the Blockade
Nearly strangled him with impersonal cold fingers.
Clever doctors saved his life. The Blockade receded.
He hopped in the Berlin streets like a cool sparrow.
His wise friends showed him a quick way to earn
Pocket-money: while English schoolboys chalked
Dirty words and sniggered behind desk-lids,
He learnt the things the words meant; his pockets
Filled up with change and his heart jingled with hate.

Now his hate has jingled in the ears of Europe.
He has taught them to know the refusal of pity.
His life is nearly over; only the darkness
Covers him as his pursuers cry over the fields.
In a moment they will tear him to pieces.

He was sick of the things that went with the dirty words:
Sick of the pocket-money and the windy street.
Then the uniforms came. They said to him: *Be Strong*.

When he was fifteen, he had a gun.
He had forgotten the Blockade and the pocket-money,
Except on nights when he could not sleep: his gun
Was a friend, but when they gave him a whip
He loved that better still. *Be strong!* He cried.

The speeches were made, the leaves fell, it was war.
To smashed Prague his gun and his whip led him in time.
There, he learnt the delight of refusing pity.

Did he never wonder about those he murdered?
Never feel curious about the severe light
That flamed in their irises as they lay dying?
Apparently not. His duty took all his care.
He fed his starving heart with cruelty
Till it got sick and died. His masters applauded.
Once, he dragged off a man's lower jaw.

Now they are coming nearer over the fields.
It is like the Blockade, only worse. He will die.
They have taken away his whip and gun.

But let us watch the scene with a true eye.
Arrest your pen, hurrying chronicler.
Do you take this for a simple act: the mere
Crushing of a pest that crawled on the world's hide?
Look again: is there not an ironic light
In the fiery sky that rings his desperate head?

He will die, this cursed man. The first pursuer
Is here. The darkness is ready to give him up.
He has, at most, a hundred breaths to draw.
But what of the cunning devil that jerked his strings?
Is that one idle, now that the strings are cut?

The man's body will rot under lime, and that soon.
But the parades have taught his uniform to march.
The hunters close in: do they feel the danger?
When they wrench his body to pieces, will they hear
A sigh as his spirit is sucked into the air
That they must breathe? And will his uniform
March on, march on, across Europe? Will their children
Hop in the streets like cool sparrows, and draw
His spirit into their hopeful lungs? Will
Their hearts jingle with hate? And who shall save them
If after all the years and all the deaths
They find a world still pitiless, a street
Where no grass of love grows over the hard stones?

JOHN WAIN

PATTERNS

I walk down the garden paths,
And all the daffodils
Are blowing, and the bright blue squills.
I walk down the patterned garden paths
In my stiff, brocaded gown.
With my powdered hair and jewelled fan,
I too am a rare
Pattern. As I wander down
The garden paths.

My dress is richly figured,
And the train
Makes a pink and silver stain
On the gravel, and the thrift
Of the borders.
Just a plate of current fashion,
Tripping by in high-heeled, ribboned shoes.
Not a softness anywhere about me,
Only whalebone and brocade.
And I sink on a seat in the shade
Of a lime tree. For my passion
Wars against the stiff brocade.
The daffodils and squills
Flutter in the breeze
As they please.
And I weep;
For the lime-tree is in blossom
And one small flower has dropped upon my bosom.

And the plashing of the waterdrops
In the marble fountain
Comes down the garden paths.
The dripping never stops.
Underneath my stiffened gown
Is the softness of a woman bathing in a marble basin,
A basin in the midst of hedges grown

So thick, she cannot see her lover hiding.
But she guesses he is near,
And the sliding of the water
Seems the stroking of a dear
Hand upon her.
What is Summer in a fine brocaded gown!
I should like to see it lying in a heap upon the ground.
All the pink and silver crumpled up on the ground.

I would be the pink and silver as I ran along the paths,
And he would stumble after,
Bewildered by my laughter.
I should see the sun flashing from his sword-hilt and the buckles
    on his shoes.
I would choose
To lead him in a maze along the patterned paths,
A bright and laughing maze for my heavy-booted lover.
Till he caught me in the shade,
And the buttons of his waistcoat bruised my body as he clasped
    me,
Aching, melting, unafraid.
With the shadows of the leaves and the sundrops,
And the plopping of the waterdrops,
All about us in the open afternoon—
I am very like to swoon
With the weight of this brocade,
For the sun sifts through the shade.

Underneath the fallen blossom
In my bosom,
Is a letter I have hid.
It was brought to me this morning by a rider from the Duke.
"Madam, we regret to inform you that Lord Hartwell
Died in action Thursday se'nnight."
As I read it in the white, morning sunlight,
The letters squirmed like snakes.
"Any answer, Madam," said my footman.
"No," I told him.

"See that the messenger takes some refreshment.
No, no answer."
And I walked into the garden,
Up and down the patterned paths,
In my stiff, correct brocade.
The blue and yellow flowers stood up proudly in the sun,
Each one.
I stood upright too,
Held rigid to the pattern
By the stiffness of my gown.
Up and down I walked,
Up and down.

In a month he would have been my husband.
In a month, here, underneath this lime,
We would have broken the pattern;
He for me, and I for him,
He as Colonel, I as Lady,
On this shady seat.
He had a whim
That sunlight carried blessing.
And I answered, "It shall be as you have said."
Now he is dead.

In Summer and in Winter I shall walk
Up and down
The patterned garden paths
In my stiff, brocaded gown.
The squills and the daffodils
Will give place to pillared roses, and to asters, and to snow.
I shall go
Up and down,
In my gown.
Gorgeously arrayed,
Boned and stayed,
And the softness of my body will be guarded from embrace
By each button, hook, and lace.

For the man who should loose me is dead,
Fighting with the Duke in Flanders,
In a pattern called a war.
Christ! What are patterns for?

AMY LOWELL

SURVIVORS

No doubt they'll soon get well; the shock and strain
    Have caused their stammering, disconnected talk.
Of course they're "longing to go out again,"—
    These boys with old, scared faces, learning to walk.
They'll soon forget their haunted nights; their cowed
    Subjection to the ghosts of friends who died,—
Their dreams that drip with murder; and they'll be proud
    Of glorious war that shatter'd all their pride . . .
Men who went out to battle, grim and glad;
Children, with eyes that hate you, broken and mad.

SIEGFRIED SASSOON
Craiglockart
October, 1917

"THEY"

The Bishop tells us: "When the boys come back
"They will not be the same; for they'll have fought
"In a just cause: they lead the last attack
"On Anti-Christ; their comrade's blood has bought
"New right to breed an honourable race.
"They have challenged Death and dared him face to face."

"We're none of us the same!" the boys reply.
"For George lost both his legs; and Bill's stone blind;
"Poor Jim's shot through the lungs and like to die;
"And Bert's gone syphilitic: you'll not find
"A chap who's served that hasn't found *some* change."
And the Bishop said: "The ways of God are strange!"

SIEGFRIED SASSOON

THE HAPPY WARRIOR

His wild heart beats with painful sobs
his strain'd hands clench an ice-cold rifle
his aching jaws grip a hot parch'd tongue
his wide eyes search unconsciously.

He cannot shriek.

Bloody saliva
dribbles down his shapeless jacket.

I saw him stab
and stab again
a well-killed Boche.

This is the happy warrior,
this is he. . . .

HERBERT READ

LAMENTATIONS

I found him in the guard-room at the Base.
From the blind darkness I had heard his crying
And blundered in. With puzzled, patient face
A sergeant watched him; it was no good trying

To stop it; for he howled and beat his chest.
And, all because his brother had gone West,
Raved at the bleeding war; his rampant grief
Moaned, shouted, sobbed and choked, while he was kneeling
Half-naked on the floor. In my belief
Such men have lost all patriotic feeling.

SIEGFRIED SASSOON

❋   ❋

MOURN NOT THE DEAD

Mourn not the dead that in the cool earth lie—
Dust unto dust—
The calm, sweet earth that mothers all who die
As all men must;

Mourn not your captive comrades who must dwell—
Too strong to strive—
Each in his steel-bound coffin of a cell,
Buried alive;

But rather mourn the apathetic throng—
The cowed and the meek—
Who see the world's great anguish and its wrong
And dare not speak!

RALPH CHAPLIN

❋   ❋

DUSK IN WAR TIME

A half-hour more and you will lean
    To gather me close in the old sweet way—
But oh, to the woman over the sea
    Who will come at the close of day?

A half-hour more and I will hear
　The key in the latch and the strong, quick tread—
But oh, the woman over the sea
　Waiting at dusk for one who is dead!

SARA TEASDALE

LOVERS, FORGET THE MOON

　　Pillowed on thoughts of war,
　　I close my eyes to sleep;
　　The moon wades through the night
　　And throngs the starry deep.

　　The light men loved of old
　　Sleeps with Endymion;
　　The moon's the airman's now—
　　Lovers, forget the moon.

CHARLES NORMAN

HOMAGE TO WREN

(*a memory of 1941*)

At sea in the dome of St. Paul's
Riding the firefull night
Fountains of sparks like a funfair,
We patrolled between the inner and outer walls,
Saw that all hatches were screwed down tight
And felt that Sir Christopher Wren had made everything
　shipshape.

Then went on deck with the spray
Of bombs in our ears and watched
The fire clouds caught in our rigging, the gaudy signals:
London Expects—but the rest of the string was vague,
Ambiguous rather and London was rolling away
Three hundred years to the aftermath of the plague,

And the flames were whippeting, dolphining, over the streets,
The red whale spouting out of submerged Londinium
And Davy Jones's locker burst wide open
To throw to the surface ledgers and lavatory seats
And all the bric-a-brac of warehouses and churches
With bones and ghosts and half forgotten quotations.

Then the storm subsided and it was dawn, it was cold,
I climbed to the crow's nest for one last look at the roaring foam,
League upon league of scarlet and gold,
But it was cold so I stretched out my hands from the drunken
   mast
And warmed my hands at London and went home.

Louis MacNeice

NIGHT BOMBERS

Aiding the moon to melt away the dark
The quiet stars flash glory through the sky.
A soulful nightingale enchants the park.
Ah, what a night! Ah, what a night to die!

For now a drone of bombers fills the sky.
A far-off siren shrieks a warning wail.
The moon heeds not, nor does the nightingale;
The white stars, if they hear, make no reply.

Shall nothing turn or stay the menacing foe?
Though thudding cannon hurl their flame-flowers high
And terror, droning terror, rides the sky,
Faint smells of apple-blossoms come and go.

The bombs have struck. A tall fire licks the sky
Above the broken walls, the crushed-in street.
Was ever bird-sung requiem more sweet?
Ah, what a night! Ah, what a night to die!

PAUL SCOTT MOWRER

THESE ARE THE BOYS

These are the boys of whom we said
　　"They are not what their fathers were;
They have no heart, and little head;
　　They slouch, and do not cut their hair."

Yet these like falcons live and die;
　　These every night have new renown;
And while we heave a single sigh
　　They shoot a brace of bombers down.

A. P. HERBERT
July 28, 1940

HEROD

No more milk at our house.
No more milk for the neighbor's girl.
No more milk for us.

And tomorrow no more bread.

Here are the days when the children will watch
Us with their big serious eyes
Eyes too big because they are hungry.
Here are the days
When the children will languish and die.

Nevertheless, nobody has said nevertheless
That this is a war for the children.
This is the war they wage on the war
The children won't have to go to twenty years from now.

Onward! good subjected peoples,
Onward! one more blow for the right.
They say the enemy children
Are already dying of hunger.

No more milk at our house
And tomorrow no more bread.

MARCEL MARTINET

THE REFUGEES

Mute figures with bowed heads
They travel along the road;
Old women, incredibly old
and a hand-cart of chattels.

They do not weep:
Their eyes are too raw for tears.

Past them have hastened
processions of retreating gunteams
baggage-wagons and swift horsemen.
Now they struggle along
with the rearguard of a broken army.

We shall hold the enemy towards nightfall
and they will move
mutely into the dark behind us,
only the creaking cart
disturbing their sorrowful serenity.

HERBERT READ

TRIUMPHAL ENTRY

He comes with conqueror's pace;
Hail, hero of the empty town!
How quiet is the market-place
Since the bombs came down.

The drums roll, the horns ring out,
And bright flags stain the air;
No children crowd the curb to shout
To see the soldiers there.

Yet empty now the schoolhouse stands,
And empty since the planes went by;
Children in school in other lands
Will mark this victory.

CHARLES NORMAN

EXODUS

They came from the terror and tumult
fleeing the bombarded provinces
where only
those bells keep tolling death
that nobody has seen and nobody heeds.
They came from the confines of a world
lost forever . . . and lost for nothing!

They brought on horseback, on foot, in hearses
or on old fire-engines
all that one saves
—in the blind moment of anguish—
of what was a home, a custom,
a landscape, a period of the soul:
a picture of a child dressed as an admiral,
the projector of a magic lantern,
a broken clock, a calendar,
the cover of an umbrella,
the hidden passport where visas bleed,
and, close to the heart, not a medal,
or a love letter, but a bundle
of banknotes—because all,
even the poorest, hoped
to buy a happy and free future
upon their arrival at the desired border.

They came without rancor, without thinking,
forming a large centipede of careful shadows,
surprised at being so numerous
at not discovering in so many faces
a kind smile, a pair of eyes
to look into, on passing, without mistrust.

They went into exile with the same
rigid step, anonymous and obscure,
which took them—during the abandoned peace—
to the workshop, to school, to the office,
asking forgiveness of each other
when the multitude crowded them
on a narrow bend
of the dusty, burning and long road.

At times a fury raged.
It was a rapid flame,
a sudden outcry which could hardly
prove up to what point lied to them
heaven, sun, wind, distances.

But soon silence returned.
Because there is nothing more silent
    than a people on the march
from dawn to exile,
on foot, on horseback, by car,
in combat cars, in ambulances,
an army which advances asking itself
at each instant if the white tower
discovered at the foot of the hill
already announces the end:
the barn where the vanquished
can finally find a dream without borders
on a soil that yesterday was a country.

JAIME TORRES BODET

THE COMPANION

She was sitting on the rough embankment,
her cape too big for her tied on slapdash
over an odd little hat with a bobble on it,
her eyes brimming with tears of hopelessness.
An occasional butterfly floated down
fluttering warm wings onto the rails.
The clinkers underfoot were deep lilac.
We got cut off from our grandmothers
while the Germans were dive-bombing the train.
Katya was her name. She was nine.
I'd no idea what I could do about her,
but doubt quickly dissolved to certainty:
I'd have to take this thing under my wing;
—girls were in some sense of the word human,
a human being couldn't just be left.
The droning in the air and the explosions

receded farther into the distance,
I touched the little girl on the elbow.
"Come on. Do you hear? What are you waiting for?"
The world was big and we were not big,
and it was tough for us to walk across it.
She had galoshes on and felt boots,
I had a pair of second-hand boots.
We forded streams and tramped across the forest;
each of my feet at every step it took
taking a smaller step inside the boot.
The child was feeble, I was certain of it.
"Boo-hoo," she'd say. "I'm tired," she'd say.
She'd tire in no time I was certain of it,
but as things turned out it was me who tired.
I growled I wasn't going any further
and sat down suddenly beside the fence.
"What's the matter with you?" she said.
"Don't be so stupid! Put grass in your boots.
Do you want to eat something? Why won't you talk?
Hold this tin, this is crab.
We'll have refreshments. You small boys,
you're always pretending to be brave."
Then out I went across the prickly stubble
marching beside her in a few minutes.
Masculine pride was muttering in my mind:
I scraped together strength and I held out
for fear of what she'd say. I even whistled.
Grass was sticking out from my tattered boots.
So on and on
we walked without thinking of rest
passing craters, passing fire,
under the rocking sky of '41
tottering crazy on its smoking columns.

YEVGENY YEVTUSHENKO

MINED COUNTRY

They have gone into the gray hills quilled with birches,
Drag now their cannon up the chill mountains;
But it's going to be long before
Their war's gone for good.

I tell you it hits at childhood more than churches
Full up with sky or buried town fountains,
Rooms laid open or anything
Cut stone or cut wood,

Seeing the boys come swinging slow over the grass
(Like playing pendulum) their silver plates,
Stepping with care and listening
Hard for hid metal's cry.

It's rightly-called-chaste Belphoebe some would miss,
Some, calendar colts at Kentucky gates;
But the remotest would guess that
Some scheme's gone awry.

Danger is sunk in the pastures, the woods are sly,
Ingenuity's covered with flowers!
We thought woods were wise but never
Implicated, never involved.

Cows in mid-munch go splattered over the sky;
Roses like brush-whores smile from bowers;
Shepherds must learn a new language; this
Isn't going to be quickly solved.

Sunshiny field grass, the woods floor, are so mixed up
With earliest trusts, you have to pick back
Far past all you have learned, to go
Disinherit the dumb child,

Tell him to trust things alike and never to stop
Emptying things, but not let them lack
Love in some manner restored; to be
Sure the whole world's wild.

RICHARD WILBUR

INNOCENTS

The falling shell, the bomb, the undiscriminating blast,
Search mouse and rat out, beetle and bird destroy;
The flaming body of man moves in a vast
Multitude of slain innocents that would enjoy
A little longer the ease of each his kind:
But man's destruction is complete and blind.

Perhaps life is given again to the untimely torn
And wrecked creatures whose unhappy lot it was
To be born in these cities we are obliterating,
For the bat and the frightened horse and the new-born
Kitten dread the falling destruction because
It is an unnatural hazard not of their enemies' creating.

KENNETH HOPKINS

DOCUMENTARY

Germany and England: September, 1939

Now no more delay. The children to country safety.
Tears all over the swastikas, tears on the lions
of England, as the trains are closed and the children press
lit bewildered breaking down faces to the panes
and wave hard; steam and current surge over the rails
threading the wet summer morning to country safety.

Cameras Berlin and cameras London: no choice
here for the mind or the heart, none even for the eye
among these lineal brothers. Surely ten key men
see, with us, both depots, and will ignore the signal.
Now, Hans and Robin, the green and pleasant motherland
of Keats and Schiller. Droning louder. Now the sirens.

ROBERT BEUM

I SIT WITH MY DOLLS

(*Composed by a little girl in a Nazi death camp*)

I sit with my dolls by the stove and dream.
I dream that my father came back.
I dream that my father is still alive.
How good it is to have a father.
I do not know where my father is.

(*Translated from the Yiddish
by* Joseph Leftwich)

TO ANOTHER POET A THOUSAND
YEARS HENCE

I write in the year called World Refugee Year.
It simply means there are people without homes,
Millions of people with no place to go,
Living in tents, barracks, mud huts;
As I implied, we are doing something about it.

We also have an organization called Save the Children.
I really believe a lot of them are being saved.
The rest died wandering the roads, or by the roadside,
Some of hunger, fatigue, many machine-gunned
As they sought safety, clogging the roads with their dolls.

Older people also died in that slanted rain;
Those who did not trudged on as refugees;
That is why, of course, this year was named for them.
I ask you to remember that the year was observed,
That we did what we could to save the children.

1960

CHARLES NORMAN

THE SAVAGE CENTURY

Child, show no surprise
When the roof buries the floor;
Retain the calm in your eyes
In the ruined corridor.

When terror rides the skies,
And horror bursts the door,
Your elders, being wise,
Will tell you: it is war.

CHARLES NORMAN

HOME

The people have got used to her
they have watched her children grow
and behave as if she were
one of them—how can they know

that every time she leaves her home
she is terrified of them
that as a German Jew she sees
them as potential enemies

Because she knows what has been done
to children who were like her own
she cannot think their future safe
her parents must have felt at home
where none cared what became of them
and as a child she must have played
with people who in later life
would have killed her had she stayed

KAREN GERSHON

THEY SAY THE LAST SUPPER IS BADLY DAMAGED

(1945)

They say the Last Supper is badly damaged—
Leonardo's, and valued at one asterisk.
They say the Renaissance sprawls on the Arno in ruins,
And St. Stephen's stands a charred and roofless husk.

Each antique name descends in a shower of souvenirs.
There are questions to ask. One asks, recalls, and ponders.
Will the rubble core of the city mock the map etched in the
brain?
The feet by some habit of the bone find their way among the
cinders?

And do you remember on the far side of the Isar a phantom village in the mist?
How in Coblenz we ate on a terrace overhanging the Rhine, with
the bees at the honey?

What we sought was always in the next street just around the corner.
Do you remember? Let us take a guided tour with our hearts as cicerone.

There were people too, were there not? And where are they?
Rafael? Anna? Denise? (Last seen going east, destination a crematorium.)
Micki and Blanca? Think. Yes, think. Each, each, each was a person.
Jacques? Margit? Hans? Erna? And who was left to sing the requiem?

They say once upon a time shepherdesses made love at Versailles,
In Florence Dante dreamed his medieval dream,
And the Lorelei haunted a rock beneath the painted castles.
Once upon a time. Say it again, *Once upon a time.*

That siren strain lured us like Ulysses.
And though Time had got there first, we could not rest.
Somewhere were the magic words—perhaps hidden in the fine print of Baedeker;
Not yet had we been forced to conclude that this Europe did not exist.

Thus we wandered through a mansion of many and elegant chambers.
There must have been a price, but we never asked who paid.
Behind the wainscoting we never discovered the bones
Thrown there by arrogance, privilege, and time-honored greed.

Now the enchantment has rubbed away, we stumble in a gutted cellar
Where lurks the feudal horror with its pimps and its obscenities.
Through the gloom we see the immemorial masonry of broken bodies,
And in the binding mortar the eyes, the hopeless eyes, the terror-stricken eyes.

SAMUEL YELLEN

XXXVI

Here dead lie we because we did not choose
   To live and shame the land from which we sprung.
Life, to be sure, is nothing much to lose;
   But young men think it is, and we were young.

A. E. Housman

THE SCHOOL BOY READS HIS ILIAD

The sounding battles leave him nodding still:
   The din of javelins at the distant wall
Is far too faint to wake that weary will
   That all but sleeps for cities where they fall.
He cares not if this Helen's face were fair,
   Nor if the thousand ships shall go or stay;
In vain the rumbling chariots throng the air
   With sounds the centuries shall not hush away.

Beyond the window where the Spring is new,
   Are marbles in a square, and tops again,
And floating voices tell him what to do,
   Luring his thought from these long-warring men,—
And though the camp be visited with gods,
He dreams of marbles and of tops and nods.

David Morton

OF LATE

"Stephen Smith, University of Iowa sophomore, burned what he
   said was his draft card"
and Norman Morrison, Quaker, of Baltimore Maryland, burned
   what he said was himself.
You, Robert McNamara, burned what you said was a concentration
of the Enemy Aggressor.
No news medium bothered to put it in quotes.

And Norman Morrison, Quaker, of Baltimore Maryland, burned
   what he said was himself.
He did it with simple materials such as would be found in your
   kitchen.
In your office you were informed.
Reporters got cracking frantically on the mental disturbance
   angle.
So far nothing turns up.

Norman Morrison, Quaker, of Baltimore Maryland, burned
   and while burning, screamed.
No tip-off. No release.
Nothing to quote, to manage to put in quotes.
Pity the unaccustomed hesitance of the newspaper editorialists.
Pity the press photographers, not called.

Norman Morrison, Quaker, of Baltimore Maryland, burned
   and was burned and said
all that there is to say in that language.
Twice what is said in yours.
It is a strange sect, Mr. McNamara, under advice to try
the whole of a thought in silence, and to oneself.

GEORGE STARBUCK

CONSCIENTIOUS OBJECTOR

I shall die, but that is all that I shall do for Death.

I see him leading his horse out of the stall; I hear the clatter
on the barn-floor.
He is in haste; he has business in Finland, business in the Balkans,
many calls to make this morning.
But I will not hold the bridle while he cinches the girth.
And he may mount by himself: I will not give him a leg up.

Though he flick my shoulders with his whip, I will not tell him
which way the fox ran.
With his hoof on my breast, I will not tell him where the black
boy lies hidden in the swamp.
I shall die, but that is all that I shall do for Death.
I am not on his pay-roll.

I will not tell him the whereabouts of my friends nor of my
enemies either.
Though he promise me much, I will not map him the route to
any man's door.
Am I a spy in the land of the living, that I should deliver men
to Death?
Brother, the password and the plans of our city are safe with me;
never through me
Shall you be overcome.

EDNA ST. VINCENT MILLAY

INTERNATIONAL CONFERENCE

To kill its enemies and cheat its friends,
Each nation its prerogative defends;
Yet some their efforts for goodwill maintain,
In hope, in faith, in patience, and in vain.

COLIN ELLIS

SPANIEL'S SERMONS

'Tis more than Spaniel's place is worth
To speak his masters ill;
As long as there is Peace on Earth
He teaches men goodwill.

But when the shells begin to fly
He calls our quarrel just
And bids us keep our powder dry
And place our God in trust.

COLIN ELLIS

THE BUTCHERS AT PRAYER
(1914)

Each nation as it draws the sword
    And flings its standard to the air
Petitions piously the Lord—
    Vexing the void abyss with prayer.

O irony too deep for mirth!
   O posturing apes that rant, and dare
This antic attitude! O Earth,
   With your wild jest of wicked prayer!

I dare not laugh . . . a rising swell
   Of laughter breaks in shrieks somewhere—
No doubt they relish it in Hell,
   This cosmic jest of Earth at prayer!

DON MARQUIS

IN HUMBLENESS

Neither malt nor Milton can
Explain to God the ways of Man:
Hobnailed troops have ever trod
Upon the flocks who know that God
Has a passion, plan, or mind,
Or that the Universe is kind.

Come flood, come war, come pestilence,
Come Man at last to Common Sense:
At last admit, in humbleness,
Whatever spire he dares erect
Of either faith or intellect
Can be but his sarcophagus;

Yet even in that iron tomb
Man stirs again, as in the womb:
Tunnels free, then, word by word,
Rebuilds, and is again interred.
Read this in the histories:
Newsweek, or Thucydides.

DANIEL G. HOFFMAN

BLESSING THE BATTLE

"Father, I call on Thee!
Clouds of the cannon smoke around me are
wreathing;
Guider of battles, I call on Thee!"
                    Korner's Prayer during Fight.

It may be that the weal of nations,
    Their honor scorned, or questioned right,
Require, indeed, no lesser umpire
    To arbitrate, than ruthless fight.

It may be that the ringing trumpet,
    And piercing fife, and sullen drum
And garments rolled in blood, and murmurs,
    Discordant, of the battle's hum;—

Shrieks of the wounded and the dying,
    The wreck of limb and waste of life,
The fury of devouring carnage,
    And all the circumstance of strife,

Are *necessary* to the order
    And comfort of this world of ours,
Which has no sweet without a bitter,
    Nor without thorns possesses flowers.

And yet when brothers murder brothers,
    To ask God's blessing on the deed—
And crave His grace where onward slaughter
    Leaves living hearts behind to bleed,

Is urging far the holy mockery,—
    Is acting farce to mercy's view;
I may be wrong, for Honor's something,—
    Man on a death-bed! What think *you?*

                    WILLIAM B. TAPPAN

FRONTIER GUARD

The barbed wire is erected and the guns deployed.
The guard patrols with winter's lead weighting his feet
and darkness is his enemy as it is mine.
The rifle on his shoulder could hail out my death
or summon his should he forget I did not call him
from his warm moonfaced Ninotchka
to this check-point where the wind ignores his challenge
and makes free with zones and frontiers,
and ice aches along his veins.
The darkness is our mutual foe. My stiff bones groan
and grumble as the cold salts my old wounds and his.
And my Ninotchka is no nearer;
she would weep as much should I personify my hate
in him and blaze it on the deadness of the night.

I could call out to him as brother, tovarich,
or friend; tell him I too have crucified my God,
and have been crucified, that what he hates I hate,
or simply that the darkness is our enemy.
But he would hear only an ambush in my voice.
For we are isolated and expendable,
making our separate tracks on the same snow,
divided, conquered by the dark that seals us in.
Ice smokes our breath with malice and the trumpet **tongue**
of fear musters a monster up behind the wire,
and I am his monster as he is mine.

We, whom our common isolation should unite,
stamp, blow, but cannot generate a common thaw,
nor furnish common law to meet our common cause,
nor wrest a common summer from the earth.
The ice attacks us and the darkness separates.
Only our challenge dares to cross the frontier line.

Tom Wright

HEARTBREAK RIDGE

Men die
To an accompaniment of aimless chatter—
Drag themselves slowly up a hill
While an imaginary line is drawn on a map.
Talks have been resumed,
But pain has never ceased.
No one will give an inch
When a world is being saved
Or lost.
The human heart
Is always bleeding to death on a hill
While somebody trumps an ace
Or dices for outer garments.

EDITH LOVEJOY PIERCE

FIGHT TO A FINISH

The boys came back. Bands played and flags were flying,
And Yellow-Pressmen thronged the sunlit street
To cheer the soldiers who'd refrained from dying,
And hear the music of returning feet.
"Of all the thrills and ardours War has brought,
This moment is the finest." (So they thought.)

Snapping their bayonets on to charge the mob,
Grim Fusiliers broke ranks with glint of steel.
At last the boys had found a cushy job.

* * *

I heard the Yellow-Pressmen grunt and squeal;
And with my trusty bombers turned and went
To clear those Junkers out of Parliament.

SIEGFRIED SASSOON

OF THE GREAT WHITE WAR

During the years when the white men fought each other,
I observed how the aged cried aloud in public places
Of honour and chivalry and the duty of the young;
And how the young ceased doing the pleasant things of youth,
And suddenly became old,
And marched away to defend the aged.

And I observed how the aged
Became suddenly young;
And mouthed fair phrases, one to the other, about the Supreme
  Sacrifice,
And turned to their account-books, murmuring gravely:
Business as Usual.
And brought out bottles of wine and drank the health
Of the young men they had sent out to die for them.

THOMAS BURKE

THE FORMALITIES

On September 2, 1945,
the battleship *Missouri*
flagged like a parade
lay anchored in Tokyo Bay and

the Japanese brass with swords
and the frock-coat detail in
silk toppers briefcases and
horn-rims like wine-bottle bottoms

walked aboard on tightropes
they had stretched inside themselves.
and pushing a separate button
for each part of each bow

rendered unto Douglas MacArthur
what was MacArthur's, and
what was God's too, MacArthur
ignoring the difference, and in

the skeletal witness of Jonathan
Wainwright come from prison, and of
A. E. Percival, British Army,
wherever *he* had come from,

and of a choir of misc available
native and allied brass in open-collar
suntans assigned by the cameras,
and of the cameras themselves—

still and moving and by flash and
previously arranged floodlighting and
with full sound equipment—the
signatures fell-to and it was

done there on God's deck there
in Tokyo Bay into which I had
watched Hewie splash burning less
than two months before with Doc

dead in the nose and O'Dell
probably blubbering a prayer and
Frankie, poor bastard, blind in his
coop di-dahing no message to Whom

and T. J. waving from the top dome
and Chico and Coxie—whoever if any
they were who wanted their medals
getting them all at last—

which is to say boys at bad luck
in their tribe and wings melting
and the photographer come. And the
fish had time in two months

to pick clean Coxie's little go-to-hell
moustache like the one I shaved off,
and Chico's tattoo and the mole on
Frankie's shin and the scapular from

O'Dell's neck and so for each in (or
out of) himself there under the keel
of the battleship *Missouri* on which
the representatives of the nations

stood witnessing how much like God
Douglas MacArthur was and what a
candidate He would make
if only He were a civilian?

JOHN CIARDI

FIVE WAYS TO KILL A MAN

There are many cumbersome ways to kill a man.
You can make him carry a plank of wood
to the top of a hill and nail him to it. To do this
properly you require a crowd of people
wearing sandals, a cock that crows, a cloak
to dissect, a sponge, some vinegar and one
man to hammer the nails home.

Or you can take a length of steel,
shaped and chased in a traditional way,
and attempt to pierce the metal cage he wears.
But for this you need white horses,
English trees, men with bows and arrows,
at least two flags, a prince and a
castle to hold your banquet in.

Dispensing with nobility, you may, if the wind
allows, blow gas at him. But then you need
a mile of mud sliced through with ditches,
not to mention black boots, bomb craters,
more mud, a plague of rats, a dozen songs
and some round hats made of steel.

In an age of aeroplanes, you may fly
miles above your victim and dispose of him by
pressing one small switch. All you then
require is an ocean to separate you, two
systems of government, a nation's scientists,
several factories, a psychopath and
land that no one needs for several years.

These are, as I began, cumbersome ways
to kill a man. Simpler, direct, and much more neat
is to see that he is living somewhere in the middle
of the twentieth century, and leave him there.

EDWIN BROCK

FUTURAMA LOVE SONG

(*after Christopher Marlowe*)

Come live with me and be my love
Under the fireball we will prove
No fallout can disturb our kiss
Nor radiation touch our bliss

That gorgeous mushroom call our home
White polished cloud our faery dome
What matter if it others harm
Contaminated we'll keep warm

Your arms that numb around me lie
Shall soon resume their amorous play
And I shall stroke your singèd hair
We'll live without a single care

We'll berries in abundance find
Hidden from radioactive wind
And drink from all the melted snow
And bless what chaos did bestow

Come live with me, be yet my love
Some new mutation we may prove
Or show that two can fear as one
While we go round the raging sun

NORMAN ROSTEN

HARRY

Harry O
Sweet warrior

Long may he keep.
He made the Bomb falleth on Hiroshima,
Then had a good night's sleep.

Harry O at eighty
Good humor hail fellow

Easy fellow, church-mellow, Harry
The genial hack from the State of Mo,
Likes his early walk, memory ajog,
Ah those dear thunderous days.

Warrior of the blaze, the mushroom,
A cross for Harry cheerful—
Sleeps well, morning bright,
He has the inner light.

NORMAN ROSTEN

AT HIROSHIMA

When we came out of the station
The houses looked old, and we wondered.

But after we had walked for a while
We came to a place with wide streets

And all the buildings were new.
Children were playing on the sidewalks,

Crying to each other in shrill voices.
Bicycles went by, jingling their bells.

But we knew we were standing
Where the end of the world began.

LINDLEY WILLIAMS HUBBELL

RETURN TO HIROSHIMA

I. BOMBARDIER

Coming out of the station he expected
To bump into the cripple who had clomped,
Bright pencils trailing, across his dreams

For fifteen years. Before setting out
He was ready to offer both his legs,
His arms, his sleepless eyes. But it seemed

There was no need: it looked a healthy town,
The people gay, the new streets dancing
In the famous light. Even the War Museum

With its photos of the blast, the well-mapped
Rubble, the strips of blackened skin,
Moved one momentarily. After all,

From the window one could watch picnickers
Plying chopsticks as before, the children
Bombing carp with rice balls. Finding not

What he had feared, he went home cured at last.
Yet minutes after getting back in bed
A wood leg started clomping, a thousand

Eyes leapt wild, and once again he hurtled
Down a road paved white with flesh. On waking
He knew he had gone too late to the wrong

Town, and that until his own legs numbed
And eyes went dim with age, somewhere
A fire would burn that no slow tears could quench.

II. PILOT

All right, let them play with it,
Let them feel all hot and righteous,
Permit them the savage joy of

Deploring my inhumanity,
And above all let them bury
Those hundred thousands once again:

I too have counted the corpses

And say this: if Captain X
Has been martyred by the poets,
Does that mean I have to weep

Over his "moments of madness"?
If he dropped the bomb, and he did,
If I should sympathize, and I do

(I too have counted the corpses),

Has anyone created a plaint
For those who shot from that red sun
Of Nineteen Forty-One? Or

Tried to rouse just one of those
Thousand Jonahs sprawled across
The iron whale-bed of Saipan Bay?

I too have counted the corpses.

And you, Tom Staines, who got it
Huddled in "Sweet Lucy" at my side,
I still count yours, regretting

You did not last to taste the
Exultation of learning that
"Perhaps nine out of ten of us"

(I too have counted the corpses)

Would not end up as fertilizer
For next spring's rice crop. I'm no
Schoolboy, but give me a pencil

And a battlefield, and I'll make you
A formula: take one away
From one, and you've got bloody nothing.

I too have counted the corpses.

III. SURVIVORS

Of the survivors there was only one
That spoke, but he spoke as if whatever
Life there was hung on his telling all,

And he told all. Of the three who stayed,
Hands gripped like children in a ring, eyes
Floating in the space his wall had filled,

Of the three who stayed on to the end,
One leapt from the only rooftop that
Remained, the second stands gibbering

At a phantom wall, and it's feared the last,
The writer who had taken notes, will
Never write another word. He told all.

LUCIEN STRYK

I AM FOR PEACE

"Man's inhumanity to man,
Makes countless thousands mourn."
Robert Burns

What's in the warlike waving plume,
And in the gorgeous standard's fold
That beckon on to envied doom
Or glorious victory, the bold;
What's in the brazen trumpet's bray
And in the spirit stirring fife
And thundering drum, that call away
The generous to the deadly strife?

What magic's in old Caesar's name,
Or his who died at Babylon—
Or his, the chief of modern fame,
Who thrones, like counters, lost and won—
Yea, what's in all the high renown
That e'er contending legions gained;
The greenest wreath, the proudest crown,
That ever poet knew or feigned,

Compared with all the certain guilt
Of murder, stamped by righteous law,
The countless tears, the rivers spilt
Of blood, the crimes and woes of war?
Compared with that impetuous tide
Of sin, which flows in dreadful wrath—
The hatred, scorn and poisonous pride
That surely follow battle's path?

Oh, why should nations, lifted up
By Christian privilege, prepare
For sister realms the bitter cup,
Whose dregs are sorrow and despair!
At empty Honor's larum wake
Force that for Right could never fail,—
For fancied insult, vengeance take,
And duel on a larger scale!

Just God! this is not in Thy plan;
The monstrous dogma's not from Thee,
That what is wrong from man to man,
In governments may venial be.
Thou ever dost transgression hate,
In highest, as in humblest place;
Nor will its penalty abate
From parliament or populace.

I loathe it all! and when I see
Gay, gladsome warriors trooping by,
With glancing steel, and bravery
Of trump and drum, I can but sigh,

That men, like children, ever seem
Still pleased and flattered with a straw,
And for Fame's splendid, empty dream,
Will court the crimes and curse of war.

WILLIAM B. TAPPAN

SONNET: TO THE CASTLE AT GORDES

Gordes, what shall we do? Shall we never have peace?
Shall we never have peace sometime on earth?
Will peace on earth never come to birth
And the people's burden of war never cease?

I see nothing but soldiers, but horses and gear,
I hear nothing but discourse of conquest and arms
I hear nothing but trumpets and battle-alarms,
Naught but blood and anger do I see, do I hear.

The princes play with our lives today;
When our lives like our goods they have stolen away
Neither power nor care will they have to restore.

Unhappy are we to live under these stars
Surrounded by evil, afflicted by war;
Theirs is the guilt; but the sorrow is ours.

OLIVIER DE MAGNY
(*Translated from the French by Scott Bates*)

Excerpt from THE BIGLOW PAPERS

Ez fer war, I call it murder,—
    There you hev it plain an' flat;
I don't want to go no furder
    Than my Testyment fer that;
God hez sed so plump an' fairly,
    Et's ez long ez it is broad
An' you've gut to git up airly
    Ef you want to take in God.

'Taint your eppyletts an' feathers
    Make the thing a grain more right;
'Taint afollerin' your bell-wethers
    Will excuse ye in His sight;
Ef you take a sword an' dror it,
    An' go stick a feller thru,
Guv'ment aint to answer for it,
    God'll send the bill to you.

Wut's the use o' meetin'-goin'
    Every Sabbath, wet or dry,
Ef it's right to go amowin'
    Feller-men like oats an' rye?
I dunno but wut it's pooty
    Trainin' round in bobtail coats,—
But it's curus Christian dooty
    This 'ere cuttin' folks's throats. . . .

Tell ye jest the eend I've come to
    Arter cipherin' plaguy smart,
An' it makes a handy sum, tu,
    Any gump could larn by heart;
Laborin' man an' laborin' woman
    Hev one glory an' one shame.
Ev'y thin' thet's done inhuman
    Injers all on 'em the same. . . .

                      JAMES RUSSELL LOWELL

OUR NEW NATIONAL HYMN

We are marching on to glory with the Bible in our hands,
We are carrying the gospel to the lost in foreign lands;
We are marching on to glory, we are going forth to save
With the zeal of ancient pirate, with the prayer of modern knave;
We are robbing Christian churches in our missionary zeal,
And we carry Christ's own message in our shells and bloody steel.
By the light of burning roof-trees they may read the Word of
   Life,
In the mangled forms of children they may see the Christian
   strife.
We are healing with the Gatling, we are blessing with the sword;
For the Honor of the Nation and the Glory of the Lord.

Then march on, Christian soldiers! with word and torch in hand,
And carry free salvation to each benighted land!
Go, preach God's Love and Justice with steel and shot and shell!
Go, preach a future Heaven and prove a present Hell!
Baptize with blood and fire, with every gun's hot breath
Teach them to love the Father, and make them free in Death;
Proclaim the newer gospel, the cannon giveth peace,
Christ rides upon the warship his army to increase.
So bless them with the rifle and heal them with the sword,—
For the Honor of the Nation and the Glory of the Lord!

WILLIAM G. EGGLESTON

ON A SOLDIER FALLEN IN THE
PHILIPPINES

Streets of the roaring town,
Hush for him, hush, be still!
He comes, who was stricken down
Doing the word of our will.

Hush! Let him have his state,
Give him his soldier's crown.
The grist of trade can wait
Their grinding at the mill,
But he cannot wait for his honor, now the trumpet has been
blown;
Wreathe pride now for his granite brow, lay love on his breast
of stone.

Toll! Let the great bells toll
Till the clashing air is dim.
Did we wrong this parted soul?
We will make it up to him.
Toll! Let him never guess
What work we set him to.
Laurel, laurel, yes;
He did what we bade him do.
Praise, and never a whispered hint but the fight he fought was
good;
Never a word that the blood on his sword was his country's own
heart's-blood.

A flag for the soldier's bier
Who dies that his land may live;
O, banners, banners here,
That he doubt not nor misgive!
That he heed not from the tomb
The evil days draw near
When the nation, robed in gloom,
With its faithless past shall strive.
Let him never dream that his bullet's scream went wide of its
island mark,
Home to the heart of his darling land where she stumbled and
sinned in the dark.

WILLIAM VAUGHN MOODY

DISARMAMENT

"Put up the sword!" The voice of Christ once more
Speaks, in the pauses of the cannon's roar,
O'er fields of corn by fiery sickles reaped
And left dry ashes; over trenches heaped
With nameless dead; o'er cities starving slow
Under a rain of fire; through wards of woe
Down which a groaning diapason runs
From tortured brothers, husbands, lovers, sons
Of desolate women in their far-off homes,
Waiting to hear the step that never comes!
O men and brothers! let that voice be heard.
War fails, try peace; put up the useless sword!

Fear not the end. There is a story told
In Eastern tents, when autumn nights grow cold,
And round the fire the Mongol shepherds sit
With grave responses listening unto it:
Once, on the errands of his mercy bent,
Buddha, the holy and benevolent,
Met a fell monster, huge and fierce of look,
Whose awful voice the hills and forests shook.
"O son of peace!" the giant cried, "thy fate
Is sealed at last, and love shall yield to hate."

The unarmed Buddha looking, with no trace
Of fear or anger, in the monster's face,
In pity said: "Poor fiend, even thee I love."
Lo! as he spake the sky-tall terror sank
To hand-breadth size; the huge abhorrence shrank
Into the form and fashion of a dove;
And where the thunder of its rage was heard,
Circling above him sweetly sang the bird:
"Hate hath no harm for love," so ran the song;
"And peace unweaponed conquers every wrong!"

JOHN GREENLEAF WHITTIER

TELL BRAVE DEEDS OF WAR

"Tell brave deeds of war."

Then they recounted tales,—
"There were stern stands
"And bitter runs for glory."

Ah, I think there were braver deeds.

STEPHEN CRANE

THERE WAS CRIMSON CLASH OF WAR

There was crimson clash of war.
Lands turned black and bare;
Women wept;
Babes ran, wondering.
There came one who understood not these things.
He said, "Why is this?"
Whereupon a million strove to answer him.
There was such intricate clamor of tongues,
That still the reason was not.

STEPHEN CRANE

WAR IS KIND

Do not weep, maiden, for war is kind.
Because your lover threw wild hands
    toward the sky
And the affrighted steed ran on alone,
Do not weep.
War is kind.

Hoarse, booming drums of the regiment,
Little souls who thirst for fight,
These men were born to drill and die.
The unexplained glory flies above them,
Great is the battle-god, great, and his
    kingdom—
A field where a thousand corpses lie.

Do not weep, babe, for war is kind.
Because your father tumbled in the yellow
    trenches,
Raged at his breast, gulped and died,
Do not weep.
War is kind.

Swift blazing flag of the regiment,
Eagle with crest of red and gold,
These men were born to drill and die.
Point for them the virtue of slaughter,
Make plain to them the excellence of killing
And a field where a thousand corpses lie.

Mother whose heart hung humble
    as a button
On the bright splendid shroud
    of your son,
Do not weep.
War is kind.

STEPHEN CRANE

THE SOUDANESE

They wrong'd not us, nor sought 'gainst us to wage
The bitter battle. On their God they cried
For succour, deeming justice to abide
In heaven, if banish'd from earth's vicinage.
And when they rose with a gall'd lion's rage,

We, on the captor's, keeper's, tamer's side,
We, with the alien tyranny allied,
We bade them back to their Egyptian cage.
Scarce knew they who we were! A wind of blight
From the mysterious far north-west we came.
Our greatness now their veriest babes have learn'd,
Where, in wild desert homes, by day, by night,
Thousands that weep their warriors unreturn'd,
O England, O my country, curse thy name!

WILLIAM WATSON

GREAT POWERS CONFERENCE

The blind men add the figures, draw the maps.
The deaf men blow the bugles, beat the drums.
And peace becomes a wavering perhaps,
And war a tidal wave that goes and comes.

The legless men march forward to success,
The armless men cry: "Victory within reach!"
And life becames a length of more or less,
With sure uncertainty for all and each.

The men without a heart dispense relief,
The mindless men devise the master plan.
The perfect government ensues, in brief
The Commonwealth of Man without the man.

EDITH LOVEJOY PIERCE

REMEMBERING THAT ISLAND

Remembering that island lying in the rain
(Lost in the North Pacific, lost in time and the war)
With a terrible fatigue as of repeated dreams
Of running, climbing, fighting in the dark,
I feel the wind rising and the pitiless cold surf
Shaking the headlands of the black north.

And the ships come in again out of the fog—
As real as nightmare I hear the rattle of blocks
When the first boat comes down, the ghostly whisper of feet
At the barge pier—and wild with strain I wait
For the flags of my first war, the remembered faces,
And mine not among them to make the nightmare safe.

Then without words, with a heavy shuffling of gear,
The figures plod in the rain, in the seashore mud,
Speechless and tired; their faces, lined and hard,
I search for my comrades, and suddenly—there—there—
Harry, Charlie, and Bob, but their faces are worn, old,
And mine is among them. In a dream as real as war

I see the vast stinking Pacific suddenly awash
Once more with bodies, landing on all beaches,
The bodies of dead and living gone back to appointed places,
A ten year old resurrection,
And myself once more in the scourging wind, waiting, waiting
While the rich orators and the lying famous corrupt
Senators mine our lives for another war.

THOMAS McGRATH

THE OLD MEN AND THE YOUNG MEN

Said the old men to the young men,
  "Who will take arms to be free?"
Said the young men to the old men,
  "We."

Said the old men to the young men,
  "It is finished. You may go."
Said the young men to the old men,
  "No."

Said the old men to the young men,
  "What is there left to do?"
Said the young men to the old men,
  "You."

WITTER BYNNER

FOR AND AGAINST

I am for those who lie
Where the green tides mass;
The tumbled rows of dead
Lapped by wave or grass;
For all light lads who die
Heavier with lead;

Against all those who prowl
The jungles of their minds
For cars, stocks, bonds; for pay,
And paper of all kinds;
Who, with a Sunday soul,
On Mondays turn to prey;

With labels handy to
Fasten on you and me,
If in a stock or bond
Prodded uncomfortably;
But, unlike me or you,
Occasionally abscond.

I am for soldiers; they
Want only what they miss,
Which, as you can guess,
Is somebody to kiss,
To love, to kiss, to say
Between kisses, "Yes."

CHARLES NORMAN

SONG FOR THE HEROES

I wonder sometimes if the soldiers lying
under the sod, wrapped in their coats like beggars
sleeping under an arch, their hands filled with leaves
could take vengeance for once on the men who sent them,
coming back like beggars, seeing the homes and fields
that their obedience lost to them, the men of all countries

whether they would have anything to say
as ghosts at frosty windows to sons or brothers
other than this—"Obedience is death."
If you are willing to die, then choose obedience.

"We who are here now, men of all nations,
our hands are full of twigs, stones on our eyes,
half-afraid of what we have done (but that is forgotten

a short wild dream, when we were other men
not ourselves—but now we are ourselves again
tradesmen, farmers, students—it is we who are telling you)

you must choose carefully, for your life, and not only your life
will depend on it, in years or days, between believing
like us, that by obedience you could help or profit

the land, the fields, the people; and saying "Death is obedience."

"Because we know now that every cause is just
and time does not discriminate between the aggressor
and the dead child, the Regrettable Necessity

And the foul atrocity—the grass is objective
And turns all citizens into green mounds—
we have had time, as soldiers always have time,

resting before Plataea or Dunkirk or Albuhera
to think about obedience—though we will still spring up
at the whistle; it is too late to withdraw—that someone must
    pay
for all this, and it will be the people.

"We have nothing to tell you but this: to choose carefully
and if you still must obey, we are ready,
your fathers, grandfathers, great-grandfathers, to find you

a place at our dry table, to greet you as soldiers
with a dry nod, and sit, elbow to elbow
silently for always under the sky of soil:

but know you are choosing. When they begin to appeal
to your better nature, your righteous indignation,
your pity for men like yourselves, stand still,

look down and see the lice upon your hide.

"It may be that you, or else your children, at last
will put down your hand and crush them. But if not
remember that we are waiting, good men as you,

not fools, but men who knew the price of obeying,
the lice for what they were, the Cause for a fraud,
hoped for no good and cherished no illusions;

and we will see your mounds spring up in clusters
beside our own, and welcome you with a nod,
crucified like us all, all fellow-ghosts together,
not fooled by the swine, but going with open eyes.

"You have only to speak once—they will melt like smoke,
you have only to meet their eyes—they will go
howling like devils into bottomless death

but if you choose to obey, we shall not blame you
for every lesson is new. We will make room for you
in this cold hall, where every cause is just.

Perhaps you will go with us to frosty windows
putting the same choice as the years go round
eavesdropping when the Gadarenes call our children

or sit debating—when will they disobey?

wrapped in our coats against the impartial cold."
All this I think the buried men would say
clutching their white ribs and their rusted helmets

nationless bones, under the still ground.

ALEX COMFORT

THE VOICES OF PEACE ARE HUSHED

I have listened to men
Talking of war
And of the evils of war—
I have listened to men
Talking, talking:
My flesh is stone to the core.
The voices of peace are hushed
As children
Whose zeal is crushed

By the flinty hand of rebuff.
I have listened to men
Talking of war.
I am stone:
I can listen no more.

SOPHIE HIMMELL

THE PREVIEW

THE GHOUL-ANGELS WHO ANGELED THE LAST BIG
SHOW ANNOUNCE A NEW PRODUCTION—
A STIRRING SEQUEL TO THE RECENT MAKER OF
STARS AND HEROES.

What say the impresarios . . . the commentators?
Yes—what of the thinkers of our thoughts?
The speakers of our lines? The prompters?
Who are the sponsors? Who are the statesmen-to-be?

The spotlight darts about like a lost pup
sniffing at every heel.
The spotlight wanders like a drunk amnesiac.

They are looking for a slogan, they are
looking for a title . . . they are looking for a cause.

They are casting now.
The props are ready. The box office is manned.

Darkness whispers behind the curtain.
Fear watches from the wings with catching eyes.
Ominous music.
Someone smells smoke.

Somebody dies. Somebody dies. Somebody dies. . . .

WALTER BENTON

THE OLD PILOT'S DEATH

He discovers himself on an old airfield.
He thinks he was there before,
but rain has washed out the lettering of a sign.
A single biplane, all struts and wires,
stands in the long grass and wildflowers.
He pulls himself into the narrow cockpit
although his muscles are stiff
and sits like an egg in a nest of canvas.
He sees that the machine gun has rusted.
The glass over the instruments
has broken, and the red arrows are gone
from his gas gauge and his altimeter.
When he looks up, his propeller is turning,
although no one was there to snap it.
He lets out the throttle. The engine catches
and the propeller spins into the wind.
He bumps over holes in the grass,
and he remembers to pull back on the stick.
He rises from the land in a high bounce
which gets higher, and suddenly he is flying again.
He feels the old fear, and rising over the fields
the old gratitude. In the distance, circling
in a beam of late sun like birds migrating,
there are the wings of a thousand biplanes.
He banks and flies to join them.

In memory of Philip Thompson, d. 1960

DONALD HALL

AN AIRSTRIP IN ESSEX, 1960

It is a lost road into the air.
It is a desert
among sugar beets.
The tiny wings
of the Spitfires of nineteen-forty-one
flake in the mud of the Channel.

Near the road a brick pillbox
totters under a load of grass,
where Home Guards waited
in the white fogs of the invasion winter.

Goodnight, old ruined war.

In Poland the wind rides on a jagged wall.
Smoke rises from the stones; no, it is mist.

DONALD HALL

A POEM TO DELIGHT MY FRIENDS WHO LAUGH AT SCIENCE-FICTION

That was the year
the small birds in their frail and delicate battalions
committed suicide against the Empire State,
having, in some never-explained manner,
lost their aerial radar, or ignored it.

That was the year
men and women everywhere stopped dying natural deaths.
The aged, facing sleep, took poison;

the infant, facing life, died with the mother in childbirth;
and the whole wild remainder of the population,
despairing but deliberate, crashed in auto accidents
on roads as clear and uncluttered as ponds.

That was the year every ship on every ocean,
every lake, harbor, river, vanished without trace;
and even ships docked at quays
turned over like wounded animals, harpooned whales, or Nor-
mandies.

Yes, and the civilian transcontinental planes
found, like the war-planes, the sky-lanes crowded
and, praising Icarus, plunged to earth in flames.

Many, mild stay-at-homes, slipped in bathtubs,
others, congenital indoors-men, descending stairs,
and some, irrepressible roisterers, playing musical chairs.
Tots fell from scooter cars and tricycles
and casual passersby were stabbed by falling icicles.

Ah, what carnage! It was reported
that even bicarb and aspirin turned fatal
and seconal too, to those with mild headaches,
Whose stomachs were slightly acid, or who found they could not
sleep.
All lovers died in bed, as all seafarers on the deep.

Till finally the only people left alive
were the soldiers sullenly spread on battlefields
among the shell-pocked hills and the charred trees.
Thus, even the indispensable wars died of ennui.

But not the expendable conscripts: they remained as always.
However, since no transport was available anywhere,
and home, in any case, was dead, and bare,
the soldiers wandered eternally
in their dazed, early-Chirico landscapes,
like drunken stars in their shrinking orbits
round and round and round and round

and (since I too died in the world-wide suicide)
they may still, for all I know, be there.
Like forsaken chessmen abandoned by paralyzed players,
they may still be there,
may still be there.

EDWIN ROLFE

THE CHOICE

I have known one bound to a bed by wrist and ankle,
Scarred by the whips of a wasting ache,
Who, at the point of entering of the needle,
Looked once around to take
The final view, then spoke;
The echo of that terribly witty joke
Pursued the surgeon to his home in Kew,
Deafened a nurse all night, and leaden lay
On the heart of a thick-skinned anesthetist
Long after they'd dispatched his ended clay.

That one lies in Oxford and is its earth.
Also, a bright-eyed woman in Germany,
In a sightless trap, far below ground,
Of which another held the key,
Surveyed without visible alarm
Or twitching of a pinioned arm
The instruments set out upon a table;
Then from her mouth there flowed a resolute
Stream of satire deliciously edged until
The tormentor tormented stopped it with a boot.

She fell as ash, not bones, in Dachau fields.
All brave men breathe her when the wind
Blows east from Danube. And Tom Caine,
When the *Imperial* was mined

And water had flooded all but the wireless room,
Spoke without audible gloom
From fifty fathoms down for fifteen hours
To his messmates on land, told several stories,
Then to a doctor carefully described
Asphyxiation's onset and his doom.

He is grown water and surrounds the pole.
If ever you dip a cup in any sea
Tom Caine is in it somewhere. On the whole
Men die asleep or else disgracefully;
But not all men. Perhaps we are never,
By any average mountain, wood, or river,
More than a heart's breadth from the dust
Of one who laughed with nothing left to lose.
Who saw the joke beneath the mammoth's foot?
And what shall I choose, if I am free to choose?

HILARY CORKE

THE LAST CAMPAIGN

In the hot valley of the never was
This crumbling army stands, dry, mummified,
The cornet raising to his lips the horn
That never sounded, and a thousand hands
Clenching the hilts of swords they never raised,
Ranks of dead cavalry staring into nothing.

Strong liquor, songs shouted around the campfire
And excellent weather marked the setting out
Of this campaign against the powers of darkness,
And men from every village that they passed
Came out to join their ranks. For many weeks
They journeyed, for long months in fact across

The sunlit plateau and began to curse
The cloudless weather and demand a battle,
And every time they saw pale smoke at dusk
Rise from behind a hill, the veterans sniffed
With pleasure, stared hard through the twilight haze
And rode around the bend with sabres ready,
But always men in their own uniform
Rode out to join them.
               So this cavalcade
Rode finally into the fatal valley,
Saw from the other end approaching them
A distant cloud of dust, sparkling with points,
(Was it the gleam of weapons?) and discerned
A barely audible thunder (Was it hooves?)
And headlong rode towards the cloud of dust
Which spread out and became a vast concourse
Of horsemen spurring sweating horses on.
Headlong they rode against the enemy,
Then saw they charged an image of themselves,
A mere reflection in an airy mirror—
And men, plumes, horses, suddenly all froze.

And so this army still stands in the valley,
The gold braid and black ostrich feathers crumbling
Of riders who still hold the fraying reins
Of horses with their hooves raised in mid air.

                                GEOFFREY LEHMANN

DEATH, LOOK TO YOUR DOMAIN

I am sick of the horror of men,
Who hate their own kind most;
The earth is three-fourths ruin—
One day it will be all ghost.

It will range through the sky like a skull,
Washed by the wind and the rain—
Since men can outdo death,
Death, look to your domain.

CHARLES NORMAN

ON A MILITARY GRAVEYARD

Stranger, when you come to Washington
Tell them that we lie here
Obedient to their orders.

KENNETH REXROTH
(*After Simonides*)

SHAME

It is a cramped little state with no foreign policy,
Save to be thought inoffensive. The grammar of the language
Has never been fathomed, owing to the national habit
Of allowing each sentence to trail off in confusion.
Those who have visited Scusi, the capital city,
Report that the railway-route from Schuldig passes
Through country best described as unrelieved.
Sheep are the national product. The faint inscription
Over the city gates may perhaps be rendered,
"I'm afraid you won't find much of interest here."
Census-reports which give the population
As zero are, of course, not to be trusted,
Save as reflecting the natives' flustered insistence
That they do not count, as well as their modest horror
Of letting one's sex be known in so many words.
The uniform grey of the nondescript buildings, the absence
Of churches or comfort-stations, have given observers

An odd impression of ostentatious meanness,
And it must be said of the citizens (muttering by
In their ratty sheepskins, shying at cracks in the sidewalk)
That they lack the peace of mind of the truly humble.
The tenor of life is careful, even in the stiff
Unsmiling carelessness of the border-guards
And *douaniers,* who admit, whenever they can,
Not merely the usual carloads of deodorant
But gypsies, g-strings, hasheesh, and contraband pigments.
Their complete negligence is reserved, however,
For the hoped-for invasion, at which time the happy people
(Sniggering, ruddily naked, and shamelessly drunk)
Will stun the foe by their overwhelming submission,
Corrupt the generals, infiltrate the staff,
Usurp the throne, proclaim themselves to be sun-gods,
And bring about the collapse of the whole empire.

RICHARD WILBUR

GONE AWAY BLUES

Sirs, when you are in your last extremity,
When your admirals are drowning in the grass-green sea,
When your generals are preparing the total catastrophe—
I just want you to know how you can not count on me.

> *I have ridden to hounds through my ancestral halls,*
> *I have picked the eternal crocus on the ultimate hill,*
> *I have fallen through the window of the highest room,*
> *But don't ask me to help you 'cause I never will.*

Sirs, when you move that map-pin how many souls must dance?
I don't think all those soldiers have died by happenstance.
The inscrutable look on your scrutable faces I can read at a
*   glance—*
And I'm cutting out of here at the first chance.

I have been wounded climbing the second stair,
I have crossed the ocean in the hull of a live wire,
I have eaten the asphodel of the dark side of the moon,
But you can call me all day and I just won't hear.

O patriotic mister with your big ear to the ground,
Sweet old curly scientist wiring the birds for sound,
O lady with the Steuben glass heart and your heels so rich and
round—
I'll send you a picture postcard from somewhere I can't be found.

I have discovered the grammar of the Public Good,
I have invented a language that can be understood,
I have found the map of where the body is hid,
And I won't be caught dead in your neighborhood.

O hygienic inventor of the bomb that's so clean,
O lily white Senator from East Turnip Green,
O celestial mechanic of the money machine—
I'm going someplace where nobody makes your scene.

Good-by, good-by, good-by,
Adios, au 'voir, so long,
Sayonara, dosvedanya, ciao,
By-by, by-by, by-by.

THOMAS McGRATH

EARTH

(With apologies to *The New Yorker*)

"A planet doesn't explode of itself," said drily
The Martian astronomer, gazing off into the air—
"That they were able to do it is proof that highly
Intelligent beings must have been living there."

JOHN HALL WHEELOCK

ABOUT THE POETS

ALBIZZI, NICCOLO DEGLI, was an Italian poet. Dante Gabriel Rossetti, the translator (1828–1882), was poet, painter, and brother of Christina Rossetti.

BACON, LEONARD (1887–1954) was noted as a satirist. He taught English at the University of California from 1910–1923, and won the Pulitzer Prize for poetry in 1941. A great-aunt, Delia Bacon (d. 1859), was a novelist and dramatist.

BARNES, KEITH, an English poet, studied at the Royal Academy of Music, among other places, and has lived on the continent and in Berkeley, California. His work has appeared in numerous magazines and has been broadcast over the BBC and in New York.

BEUM, ROBERT (1929–   ) is a native of Mount Vernon, Ohio, and was graduated from Ohio State University in 1952. He has written magazine articles and textbooks, in addition to poetry, and teaches at Creighton University.

BODET, JAIME TORRES, Mexican educator and poet, has been director-general of UNESCO and minister of education in his native land.

BRINNIN, JOHN MALCOLM (1916–   ) was born in Nova Scotia and is a graduate of the University of Michigan. He is poet, teacher, editor, and lecturer.

BROCK, EDWIN, is the author of "Five Ways to Kill a Man," which first appeared in *The Listener*, an English magazine. His latest book of poems is *With Love from Judas*.

BROOKE, RUPERT (1887–1915) is perhaps the most famous of all the poets who died during World War I. He is buried on an island in the Aegean.

BURKE, THOMAS (1886–1945) is perhaps best known for one of his Limehouse stories, "Broken Blossoms."

BYNNER, WITTER (1881–   ) was born in Brooklyn and is a graduate of Harvard. A playwright and former president of the Poetry Society of America, he is noted, among other things, for his part in the *Spectra* hoax, which "created" a nonexistent school of poetry.

CAVAFY, CONSTANTINE P. (1863–1933) is one of the greatest of the modern Greek poets. His first collection appeared in 1904. The poem by which he is represented here was translated by Rae Dalven, a native of Greece who now lives in New York.

CHAPLIN, RALPH, a leader of the International Workers of the World, was jailed during World War I for his antiwar beliefs.

CHINESE POETS, THE: Chang Chi. Ch'en Tao. Hsu Chao. Li Po. Shen Ch'üan-ch'i. Ts-Ao Sung. Tu Fu. Wang Han. Wang Tsan.

CIARDI, JOHN (1916–   ) was born in Boston and has been poet, essayist, lecturer, television personality, and poetry editor of *Saturday Review*. He also was a gunner on a B-29 during World War II. Ciardi says he gave up teaching "because I found my own papers more interesting to work on than those of my students, and because I thought of a tax problem as more interesting than planned poverty."

COMFORT, DR. ALEX (1920–   ) was jailed in 1962, with others including Bertrand Russell, for organizing a sitdown in Trafalgar Square to protest the use of nuclear weapons. He is a physician and native Londoner.

CORKE, HILARY (1921–   ) was born in Malvern, England, collects rock crystal and ancient coins, and is married to a granddaughter of Robert Bridges.

CRANE, STEPHEN (1871–1900), although principally known for such prose masterpieces as *The Red Badge of Courage,* also wrote poetry which was as stamped with realism as were his stories. He was a war correspondent in Greece and Cuba.

CUMMINGS, E. E. (1894–1962) was a native of Cambridge, Mass., who joined an American volunteer ambulance corps in World War I before the United States entered that conflict. He was confined to a French concentration camp for several months on a charge (later disproved) that he had engaged in treasonable correspondence. Cummings was poet, novelist, and painter.

DAVIDSON, DONALD (1893–   ) served in the 81st Division during World War I and saw action in the Meuse–Argonne offensive. He has written poetry and prose, been editor and teacher. Now a professor at Vanderbilt University, Davidson is a native of Campbellsville, Tenn.

DAWE, BRUCE (1930–   ) was born in Geelong, Victoria, and is now with the Royal Australian Air Force. He studied at Melbourne

University after having worked as a farmhand, millhand, copyboy, gardener, and postman.

DEUTSCH, BABETTE (1895–   ), once secretary to Thorstein Veblen, has taught poetry and done translations from the Russian and German with her husband, Avrahm Yarmolinsky, as well as written poetry, novels, and biography. She was born in New York City.

DOUGLAS, KEITH (1900–1924) is regarded by many as the finest poet of World War II. He was born in Tunbridge Wells, Kent, and died in Normandy 24 years later after having been mentioned in dispatches for a daring raid behind enemy lines. He had left Oxford as an undergraduate. His mother wrote after his death: "He might have stayed in a safer spot. But I understand he couldn't. He always loathed the 'safety first' idea, holding that one might as well be dead as afraid to move. . . ."

EGGLESTON, WILLIAM G., seemingly, was a Southern poet. At least his poem protesting the Spanish-American War first appeared in the Asheville, North Carolina, Sunday *Republican* on September 27, 1899.

ELLIS, COLIN, held the rank of lieutenant during World War I. In France he was a forward observation officer at the capture of Vimy Ridge, for which he was awarded the British Military Cross. His first book of verse, *The Dispassionate Pilgrim,* was published in 1927.

ENGLISH, MAURICE, is a native of Chicago, and was graduated from Harvard in 1933. He was a reporter and foreign correspondent before becoming a senior editor of the University of Chicago Press.

ETTER, DAVE (1928–   ) was born in California and now is assistant editor with the Encyclopaedia Britannica. He majored in history at the University of Iowa and has hitchhiked over much of the United States. His poems have appeared in more than fifty magazines.

EVERSON, WILLIAM (1912–   ) is a native of Sacramento, California, who has been better known as Brother Antoninus since he joined a Dominican order in 1951 as a lay brother. During World War II he established a handpress in the Oregon camp where he was confined as a conscientious objector.

FRANCIS, ROBERT CHURCHILL (1901–   ) was born in Upland, Pennsylvania, and now lives near Amherst, Massachusetts. He is a graduate of Harvard, and during 1957–58 was in Rome on a fellowship from the American Academy of Arts and Letters. He says that "writing, reading, music, and gardening" take up most of his time.

FREEMAN, ARTHUR (1938–   ) is a professor of English and contributor to numerous magazines who was born in Cambridge, Mass.

GASCOYNE, DAVID (1916–   ) is a native of Middlesex, England, who lived for some years in France. He also stayed in the United States for several months during 1952.

GERSHON, KAREN. All one needs to know of this poet is that she was one of the Jewish children brought to England before World War II whose parents later died in the Nazi death camps.

GIBSON, WILFRID WILSON (1878–1962) was born in Northumberland, England, and had written 22 books of poetry by the time he was 50. He has been called "the poet of the industrial poor."

GILLMAN, RICHARD, had his first book of poems published in 1965 after Rolfe Humphries brought his work to the attention of that friend-of-the-poet, Alan Swallow, of Denver. Gillman then was director of the office of public affairs at Brandeis University.

GRAVES, ROBERT (1895–   ) first came into prominence through his World War I poetry, although his published works now number more than 100. He lives on the island of Majorca, and is a classical scholar.

GUITERMAN, ARTHUR (1871–1943) is perhaps best-known for his comic verse. He was born in Vienna of American parents and was registered at the United States consulate there to ensure his American citizenship. He was a champion sprinter—and Phi Beta Kappa—at the College of the City of New York.

HACKER, MARY, as you may suspect from her poem, has two sons (and a daughter). She is a Londoner now living in Harpenden, Hertfordshire.

HALL, DONALD (1928–   ) was born in New Haven, Conn., and attended Harvard and Oxford. His first book, *Exiles and Marriages,* appeared while he was a Junior Fellow at Harvard and was the Lamont Poetry Selection for 1955 of the Academy of American Poets. He was poetry editor of *Paris Review* for several years.

HARDY, THOMAS (1840–1928) was best known as a novelist but also wrote short stories and a great deal of poetry. He was both a realist and a pessimist.

HARTE, BRET (1836–1902) was born in Albany, New York, and died in London after his early fame had all but vanished. He was poet, short story writer, miner, and United States consul in Prussia and Scotland.

HERBERT, SIR ALAN PATRICK (1890–   ) is a British journalist and Member of Parliament who attacked the English divorce laws in 1934 with a novel, *Holy Deadlock.* The laws were revised three years later. Herbert was wounded at Gallipoli during World War I.

HIMMELL, SOPHIE, is the author of three collections of verse. Her first poetry appeared in *The New York Sun.* She was a member of the Poetry Society of America, The New York Women Poets, and The Catholic Poetry Society.

HOFFMAN, DANIEL G. (1923–   ) was graduated from Columbia University in 1947 after serving three years in the U.S. Air Force. He is a native of New York City and has taught in Europe and the United States.

HOPKINS, KENNETH (1914–   ) is a prolific and versatile writer who, under various pseudonyms, has turned out motion picture scripts, mysteries, poetry, biography, and children's books. He served in the British army during World War II and in 1961 was a visiting lecturer at the University of Texas.

HORGAN, PAUL (1903–   ) was born in Buffalo, New York, and has been librarian, novelist, historian, and poet. He won the Pulitzer Prize in 1955 for *Great River: The Rio Grande in History.*

HOUSMAN, A. E. (1859–1936) was made famous by *A Shropshire Lad,* which appeared in 1896. No other books by Housman appeared until 1922 when *Last Poems* was issued. He was a brother of Laurence Housman, novelist and poet, and a classical scholar.

HUBBELL, LINDLEY WILLIAMS (1901–   ) born in Hartford, Conn., has been with the New York Public Library since 1925. His first book of poems, *Dark Pavilion,* appeared in 1927.

HUGHES, LANGSTON (1902–1967) moved into the literary limelight in 1926 with his book of poems, *Weary Blues,* and remained there until his death. He also wrote plays, novels, short stories, and an autobiography, *The Big Sea.* His work was widely translated. A combo at his funeral played a piece Hughes had requested: "Do Nothing 'Til You Hear From Me."

JARRELL, RANDALL (1914–1966), poet, critic, teacher, and novelist, was born in Nashville and died in an auto accident. He served in the Air Force during World War II.

JEFFERS, ROBINSON (1887–1962) was noted for his narrative, dramatic, and lyric verse, often pessimistic and religious in tone. An American poet, he was born in Pittsburgh and lived his last years on the Central California coast.

LEHMANN, GEOFFREY (1940–   ) was born in Sydney, Australia, and is a lawyer. His work has appeared in many magazines.

LETTS, WINIFRED M. is an Irish writer of poetry, children's books, and plays, two of which have been performed at the Abbey Theatre in Dublin.

LEVERTOV, DENISE (1923–   ) was born in London but now lives in New York City with her American husband. She won a Guggenheim Fellowship in 1962.

LONGFELLOW, HENRY WADSWORTH (1807–1882) is the only American to be represented in Poet's Corner at Westminster Abbey. His *The Courtship of Miles Standish* sold 15,000 copies in Boston and London on publication day in 1858. He was professor of modern languages and library at Bowdoin College from 1829–35, and later taught at Harvard.

LOWELL, AMY (1874–1925) once said of herself, "I am the only member of my family who is worth a damn." And Carl Sandburg remarked, "Arguing with Amy is like arguing with a big blue wave." The cigar-smoking Miss Lowell has been widely anthologized and lightly regarded, but is remembered where many of her contemporaries have been forgotten. She was a relative of James Russell Lowell, and was awarded the Pulitzer Prize (posthumously) in 1926.

LOWELL, JAMES RUSSELL (1819–1891) was an American poet, critic, and humorist. He taught French and Spanish at Harvard, where he succeeded Henry Wadsworth Longfellow. He was the first editor of *Atlantic Monthly,* and a strong supporter of abolition.

MACAULAY, LORD THOMAS BABINGTON (1800–1859) was essayist, historian, poet, and Member of Parliament. His *History of England* still is read, and his *Lays of Ancient Rome* once were immensely popular.

MACGILL, PATRICK (1890–   ) is an Irish poet and novelist. His works include *Songs of the Dead End.*

MACNEICE, FREDERICK LOUIS (1907–   ) also has written under the pen name of Louis Malone. He is a native of Belfast, a graduate of Oxford, and is a classical scholar who taught Greek for a brief period in London. He collaborated with W. H. Auden on a book of travel sketches in verse, *Letters from Iceland,* and also has been a program director for the BBC.

MAGNY, OLIVIER DE (1529–1560) was a French poet whose works include *Les Amours, Les Gaietés, Les Soupirs,* and *Les Odes.*

MARQUIS, DONALD ROBERT PERRY (1878–1937) may be the only famous person ever born in Walnut, Illinois, and certainly is the only native of that town ever to have worked for Joel Chandler Harris on Uncle Remus's Magazine. Marquis is perhaps best-remembered for creating Archy and Mehitabel—the literary cockroach and his disreputable friend, an alley cat. Marquis was for many years a New York newspaper columnist.

MCGINLEY, PHYLLIS (1905–   ) was born in Ontario, Oregon, and is principally known as a writer of light verse. She has also done essays, children's books, and the lyrics for *Small Wonder,* a musical revue.

MCGRATH, THOMAS (1916–   ) was born on a South Dakota farm, studied at North Dakota, Louisiana State, and Oxford, and served three years in the army. He has been a farmer, college teacher, and shipyard worker. His writings include children's books, documentary films, and a novel.

MELVILLE, HERMAN (1819–1891) spent the final twenty years of his life as a customs inspector in New York City. He was the author of *Moby Dick* and other novels, and had traveled through the South Seas on whaling ships and with the United States Navy.

MILLAY, EDNA ST. VINCENT (1892–1950), a graduate of Vassar, lived for a time in Greenwich Village and wrote short stories under the nom de plume of Nancy Boyd. She wrote plays (and acted), and had the ability to write both light and serious poetry. She became politically-conscious in her later years and once wrote: "God! we could keep this planet warm by friction, if the sun should fail." She won the Pulitzer Prize in 1923 for *The Harp Weaver and Other Poems.*

MOODY, WILLIAM VAUGHN (1869–1910) was both poet and playwright. He was born in Spencer, Indiana, and taught English at the University of Chicago from 1895–99 and 1901–07.

MORTON, DAVID (1886–1957) taught English and boxing at Amherst College from 1924 to 1945. He was a Kentuckian and had worked on newspapers for six years before turning to teaching. His first book was *Ships in Harbour.* He was especially gifted as a writer of sonnets.

Moss, Stanley, a native of New York City, has written poetry for a number of magazines in the United States and England. His first book, *The Wrong Angel,* appeared in 1966.

Mourão-Ferreira, David, a Portuguese writer, also is professor, playwright, actor, editor, and critic.

Mowrer, Paul Scott, former Pulitzer Prize-winning foreign correspondent for the *Chicago Daily News,* once was described as a man who "preferred poetry to power, and meter to money."

Mullins, Helene (1899–   ), was born in New Rochelle, New York, and is both poet and novelist. When her *Balm in Gilead* was published in 1930 she was described as "something rather rare in poetry these days, being both intelligent and tuneful. Most of our intelligent poets are dry, and most of our sweet singers are silly. . . ."

Newbolt, Sir Henry (1862–1938) was an English poet and, after 1923, the official British naval historian. His best-known poem, perhaps, is "Drake's Drum," which appeared in his first book of verse, *Admirals All,* in 1897.

Norman, Charles (1904–   ) was born in Russia, came to the United States at the age of 5, went to sea as a deckhand on a freighter at 18, and later lived in Paris. He served in France during World War II. During the twelve years he was writing his biography of Christopher Marlowe, Norman also worked as writer and editor for the Associated Press, *Time* magazine, and *PM.* He became a full-time freelance writer in 1946, after the biography appeared, and now lives in New York City. He has done biographies of Shakespeare, Samuel Johnson, and Ezra Pound.

Owen, Wilfred (1893–1918), was killed on the Western Front just seven days before the Armistice and one month after winning the Military Cross. Most of his highly-regarded war poems were written during his 13 months of service in France, where he once met Siegfried Sassoon in a military hospital. He was a native of Liverpool.

Parker, Dorothy (1893–1967) was almost as famous for her verbal witticisms as for her published work. She wrote and laughed with Robert Benchley, Alexander Woollcott, James Thurber, and other legendary figures and as poet, playwright, short story writer, and critic, was widely quoted.

Pierce, Edith Lovejoy, who lives in Evanston, Illinois, is a native of England who came to the United States in 1929 and became a citizen three years later. Her poetry usually deals with religious or humanitarian themes. She studied in Paris and took extension work from the Sorbonne.

PRICE, MERLE, a co-founder of the Poetry Council of North Carolina, was born in Forest City, North Carolina, and attended Limestone College in Gaffney, South Carolina. She is a former schoolteacher and now is assistant librarian at Converse College, Spartanburg, South Carolina.

READ, SIR HERBERT (1893–   ) is the son of a Yorkshire farmer and earned the D.S.O. and Military Cross as an infantry officer in France and Belgium during World War I. He was knighted in 1953. Read was an assistant keeper at the Victoria and Albert Museum for ten years, and is an expert on ceramics and stained glass.

REED, HENRY (1914–   ) was born in Birmingham, England, and served in the Army during World War II.

REXROTH, KENNETH (1905–   ) is a native of South Bend, Indiana, who now lives in San Francisco. He is not only a poet, critic, and journalist, but has had one-man showings of his paintings in various cities, including Paris.

RICKWORD, EDGELL, was the British publisher of the *Calendar of Modern Letters* which ran in the 1920's. He was also publisher of some of D. H. Lawrence's major critical pieces.

ROLFE, EDWIN (1909–1954) also wrote *Lincoln Battalion: The Story of the Americans Who Fought in Spain.*

ROSTEN, NORMAN, American poet and playwright, won the Yale Series of Younger Poets award for his first book, *Return Again, Traveler.* He "enjoys reading his work in libraries, schools and polite bars, as well as on radio and television."

SANDBURG, CARL (1878–1967) won the Pulitzer Prize for history in 1940 for his *Abraham Lincoln: The War Years.* He was very well known as a poet, Lincoln scholar, folk song singer, and for the fog-that-came-with-little-cat-feet. Sandburg was born in Galesburg, Illinois, and spent his last years in Flat Rock, North Carolina. During his colorful career he was a milk-wagon driver, fireman, house painter, and Milwaukee and Chicago newspaperman. He served in the Sixth Illinois Volunteers in Puerto Rico in 1898.

SASSOON, SIEGFRIED (1886–1967), who will be remembered for his brilliant World War I poetry and *Memoirs of a Fox-Hunting Man,* was a captain in the Royal Welsh Fusiliers, fought in France and Palestine, and earned the Military Cross for bravery. He is said to have been the first British poet to enlist and was in uniform on August 5, 1914—the day after England declared war. He came to hate war so bitterly that he once threw one of his medals into the Mersey River as a gesture of protest.

SEEGER, ALAN (1888–1916) was killed in action on the Fourth of July, 1916, while fighting with the French army. He was a native of New York City, and his famed "Rendezvous" poem is one of the two or three best-known poems of World War I.

SELIGMAN, JOSEPH, was a member of the American "Lincoln Battalion" of the International Brigade. His poem included in this anthology was written shortly before he died, at 23 years of age, on the Jarama Front in Spain, 1937.

SIMPSON, LOUIS (1923–   ) won the Pulitzer Prize in 1964 for *At the End of the Open Road*. He is a native of Jamaica and served in a U.S. Airborne Division during World War II. He has taught at Columbia University and the University of California at Berkeley.

SLESSOR, KENNETH (1901–   ), born in New South Wales, was an official Australian war correspondent in Greece, Palestine, Syria, Egypt, and New Guinea.

SOUTHEY, ROBERT (1774–1843) was a major literary figure in his day and is a minor one now. He was poet laureate of England from 1813 until his death.

STARBUCK, GEORGE, who came out of California to study in Chicago and at Harvard, has worked at publishing in Boston, as a librarian in Buffalo, lived in Italy as a Prix de Rome winner and Guggenheim Fellow and—as of mid-1967—taught in the creative writing program at the University of Iowa.

STARRETT, VINCENT (1886–   ), who is the world authority on Sherlock Holmes, is an incurable romantic and a gentleman of a vanishing school. Poet, critic, novelist, and connoisseur of murder, Starrett was born in Canada and now lives in Chicago. He is one of the founders of the Baker Street Irregulars.

STOUTENBERG, ADRIEN, a native of Darfur, Minnesota, has been librarian, reporter, editor, and free-lance writer. She also plays the guitar, collects driftwood, and is fond of cats.

STRYK, LUCIEN, attended Indiana University, the University of Iowa, the Sorbonne, and London University, and currently teaches at Southern Illinois University. He also has studied in Iran and lectured in Japan.

TAPPAN, WILLIAM BINGHAM (1794–1849) was born in Beverly, Massachusetts, and had 11 books of poetry published.

TEASDALE, SARA (1884–1933) was awarded a special Pulitzer Prize for *Love Songs* in 1918, and the book went into five printings within the year. Miss Teasdale, who was born in St. Louis, killed herself at the age of 49. She had six books published during her lifetime and two posthumously. She had a fine lyric gift.

TREECE, HENRY (1912–   ), a native of England, was a flight lieutenant in the Royal Air Force in which he served from 1941–1946. He is novelist, poet and dramatist, and has lectured widely in the United States. Treece described himself, in 1961, as "strictly a small-town person, a family man, an ex-poet, who has been a historical novelist for the past ten years."

TRYPANIS, CONSTANTINE A. (1909–   ) was born in Chios, Greece, and now teaches at Oxford University, where he is a professor of medieval and modern Greek. He was an infantryman from 1939–1941.

UNTERMEYER, LOUIS (1885–   ) was born in New York City, and without finishing high school became vice-president of a jewelry manufacturing business. He resigned in 1923 to become a writer, editor, and lecturer. He has been poet-in-residence at several universities, and is an honorary member of Phi Beta Kappa. It may seem impertinent to anthologize so noted an anthologist, but Untermeyer is also a fine poet and parodist.

VIERECK, PETER (1916–   ) served in the psychological warfare branch of the United States Army from 1943–1945. His younger brother was killed near Anzio in 1944 while Viereck was at an army base in Carthage. He has written numerous works of prose and poetry, and is a professor at Mount Holyoke College. He won the Pulitzer Prize in 1949 for *Terror and Decorum*.

WAIN, JOHN (1925–   ) gave up teaching in 1955 to become a free-lance writer. He was born in Stoke-on-Trent, Staffordshire, and was educated at Oxford. He has lectured extensively in the United States and Europe, and has written essays and short stories as well as poetry.

WARNER, CHARLES DUDLEY (1829–1900) was essayist and editor, and helped Mark Twain write *The Gilded Age*. He was born in Plainfield, Massachusetts, and worked as a railroad surveyor and lawyer before becoming editor of the *Hartford* (Conn.) *Evening Post* in 1861.

WATSON, SIR WILLIAM (1858–1935) gave strong expression to his political beliefs in his poetry, and once wrote, ". . . if some of his readers are disposed to regret that while he has grown older his faith has not become more buoyant, he can only ask them to extend a kindly tolerance to one who, even as they, is sincere in his quest of Truth."

WHEELOCK, JOHN HALL (1886–   ) was born in Far Rockaway, New York, and studied at Harvard and the Universities of Berlin and Göttingen. He went with Charles Scribner's Sons in 1911 and later became treasurer of that firm. His first book—with a Harvard classmate, Van Wyck Brooks—was published in 1905: *Verses of Two Undergraduates.*

WHITTEMORE, REED (1919–   ) was born in New Haven and edited the *Carleton Miscellany* while teaching English at Carleton College. He was consultant in poetry at the Library of Congress in 1964–65. He became a major while serving with the U.S. Army Air Forces from 1941–45. He writes poems, essays, and short stories.

WHITTIER, JOHN GREENLEAF (1807–1892) was a dedicated abolitionist and was known as "the Quaker Poet." He is remembered for his poem "Barbara Frietchie" (1864) as well as for one of the most famous couplets in our language: "Of all sad words of tongue and pen / The saddest are these: 'It might have been.' "

WILBUR, RICHARD (1921–   ) won the Pulitzer Prize for poetry with *Things of This World,* in 1957, and a National Book Award the same year. He was born in New York City and served with the 36th Infantry Division during World War II. He has taught at Harvard and Wesleyan, and has done numerous translations including Molière's *Misanthrope.* He also collaborated with Lillian Hellman on the comic opera, *Candide.*

WOLFE, HUMBERT (1885–1940) was an English poet whose forte was satire. He was born in Italy and began writing verse at Oxford. He represented England in the international labor office at Geneva.

WRIGHT, TOM, a native of Glasgow, served in the army from 1943–1947 in Europe, Burma, India, and Japan. He is a poet, dramatist, and creator of stained-glass windows, who now makes his home in Edinburgh.

YELLEN, SAMUEL (1906–   ), a native of Lithuania, was graduated from Western Reserve and took his M.A. at Oberlin. He founded the Poetry Series of the Indiana University Press, and edited it for six years. He writes both prose and poetry and is a professor of English at Indiana University.

YEVTUSHENKO, YEVGENY (1933–   ) was born in Zima, Siberia. He achieved fame outside of Russia with his poem "Babi Yar," an attack on anti-Semitism. Yevtushenko has visited this country and appeared before college groups.

Not included in this section:

Walter Benton
Cho Sung Kyun
Marcel Martinet
Mance Williams

INDEX